Don't just take our word for it...

POWER SPENDING

GETTING MORE FOR LESS

Written by:

Carolyn Johnston
Eric Poulin
Robin Poulin

Illustrated by:

David Johnston

First Edition

ABC
PUBLISHING

Printed in the USA

Power Spending: Getting More For Less

Library and Archives Canada Cataloguing in Publication

Johnston, Carolyn, 1960-

    Power spending : getting more for less / Carolyn Johnston, Eric Poulin, Robin Poulin ; David Johnston, illustrator.

Includes index.

Issued also in an electronic format.

ISBN 978-0-9866789-0-5

    1. Finance, Personal. I. Poulin, Eric, 1975- II. Poulin, Robin, 1974- III. Johnston, David, 1984- IV. Title.

HG179.J639 2010   332.024   C2010-906194-2

All inquiries should be addressed to:

A Better Choice Publishing
41 Temperance Street, P.O. Box 2,
Clarington, ON L1C 3A0
Phone: 888-700-8414   Email: contact@abcpublishing.org
Discounts available on the purchase of 5 or more copies of this book.

First Edition—Printed in the USA

WARNING-DISCLAIMER

This book is intended to provide information about money management basics. It is also meant to provide you with money saving ideas and to point you to other resources that are available on this topic. It is sold with the understanding that the publisher and the authors are not engaged in providing financial or other professional services. Financial, legal, estate and tax issues are very unique and require personal and individual attention. We recommend that you seek the services of competent legal, financial and tax professionals when you are making financial decisions.

We have tried to make this book as complete as possible; however, there may be mistakes, both typographical and in content. The book contains information that is current only up to the printing date.

The purpose of this book is to educate and entertain. The authors and A Better Choice Publishing shall have neither liability nor responsibility to any person or entity with respect to any loss or damage caused, or alleged to have been caused, directly or indirectly, by the use of the information contained in this book or from any website mentioned in the book or listed on our website.

If you do not wish to be bound by the above, you may return this book to the publisher for a full refund.

Contents

Section II Advanced Power Spending

Acknowledgements

We give a **BIG** thank you to our editor-in-chief, Ed Poulin. He was our first and foremost sounding board on each and every chapter. He saw us through our first flawed attempts right to the much improved end. (And that's not just our opinion, Ed agrees too.) Ed, thanks for sticking with us.

A special thank you to our other "readers" who were willing to give their invaluable input:

Joanne Alter, CelebrateWithStyle.com;

Dianna Baros, TheBudgetBabe.com;

Deron Beal, Freecycle.org;

Jackie Brooks;

Annie Dorrell-Nichol;

Nancy Gibson;

Kathleen Hannaford;

Jim Harnish, SavingsNut.com;

Anne Hindley;

Doug Hoyes, MoneyProblems.ca;

Heather Jack, TheVolunteerFamily.org;

Jennifer Johnston;

Michelle Jones, CouponQueen.org;

Brad Miller, LDS Family Services;

Heather McAlpine, CFP;

Marion Morassutti;

Eric Putnam, DebtCoach.ca;

Richard Rainford, MoneySmarts4Kids.com;

Kristina Rundquist, TravelSense.org;

Carol Ann Walker, BACD.ca; and last only because his name starts with the letter Z,

Steve Zussino, GroceryAlerts.ca.

And to all those who took the time to contribute their wonderful ideas via our surveys—thank you!! Unfortunately, we don't have room to name you all, but you know who you are. You've added tremendous value to the book. We know that your ideas, stories and experiences will be beneficial to our readers. After all, nothing compares to real life experience when you want to see how theory can be put into practice.

Preface

We might as well get this over with right at the start. We're going to use the "B" word—B-U-D-G-E-T. We know that was painful, but hold on—don't worry—we want to make budgeting fun. You heard us right—budgeting and fun in the same sentence. Stop laughing! We know the two words don't usually go together but give us a chance. This book is about much more than budgeting—in fact, it is *so* much more! These pages are about what you do with your money—how you spend, save and use it more effectively.

The following pages are filled with money facts, money mistakes and money solutions, but best of all, with real people's comments. We sent out surveys and you will find some of the responses to our questions on the last page of each chapter. These pages include our respondents' ideas, recommendations and "tried and true" solutions for making money work. You'll find even more of their great ideas on our website, **PowerSpendingBook.com**.

We've divided this book into two sections. In the first section you'll find some useful information about money basics—we refer to this as the ***basic economic survival*** part. In the second section you'll find lots of ideas about how to spend money better—this is the part we refer to as ***advanced power spending***.

Before we go any further we need to let you know what this book is and what it isn't. We'll begin with this explanation. There are six areas of financial planning: cash management, risk management, investment planning, special needs planning, estate planning and tax planning. We will only cover the first area—cash management. If you need specific and individual help and advice in any of these areas we recommend that you work with a certified financial planner or other specialist.

And just what does cash management cover? Net worth, cash flow, debt management and emergency planning, for example, but also the many different ways you use your money. We'll go into more detail later—we don't want to spoil the surprise!!

So, what's in it for you? That's always the bottom line. We are offering you fun, facts and freedom! When you implement the strategies that we provide in this book, you'll make better money decisions; you'll be in control of your money—not the other way around. In fact, that's how we came up with the title of our book, *Power Spending: Getting More For Less*. That's our motto, and our goals for you are first, economic survival, and then economic prosperity!!

This book shares President Lincoln's philosophy: it is "of the people, by the people, for the people." With that in mind we invite you to continue to share your great ideas with us. Let us know how you *power spend* by adding your comments at PowerSpendingBook.com. This book, and our website, are meant to be resources that are current and up-to-date and that will continue to provide you with the best "true blue, tried and tested, real life" ways to use your money better.

Each chapter includes sidebars that will bring some added insight to the topic. We've gathered financial statistics, more detailed examples or explanations (of the text material) and words of wisdom. We've divided these sidebars into 10 main categories. Each sidebar category has an icon so it can be easily identified. We are including a legend so that you can easily recognize each category when you see the icon.

Legend

These icons will be found in every chapter:

 Right On The Money
(history of money/currencies, money facts and statistics)

 Your Money's Worth
(good buys)

 Makes Cents
(money saving ideas, budgeting tips)

 Fool's Gold
(money mistakes, financial extravagances)

 Common Cents
(money quotations)

 Money Talks
(a history and explanation of money phrases)

These will appear as needed:

 Buyer Beware
(financial pitfalls to avoid)

 Factor This In
(added bits of info that we feel are helpful or interesting)

 Do The Math
(financial calculations or math related items)

 Bank On It
(nonfinancial advice that we believe you can "take to the bank")

Meet The Munneys

We want to introduce you to the young couple that will be making the journey with you through this book: Bill and Penny Munney. You will notice that they have questions throughout the chapters, which we will answer. (We refer to them at our meetings as the *talking heads*.) We're asking you to laugh along with us as we reveal some of their less-than-stellar financial moments captured in cartoon form.

Bill Munney, Penny Munney

The Munney Family

They call each other "honey,"
And help us learn 'bout money,
They're altogether funny.
The Munney Family.

You'll see they ask some questions,
We'll help them learn some lessons,
In "Power Spending" sessions.
The Munney Family.

They're here in every chapter,
We hope they cause you laughter,
With them you'll learn much faster.
The Munney Family.

Section I

Basic Economic Survival

Chapter 1
Keeping Up With The Joneses
MONEY PSYCHOLOGY

"But I need it...and it's on sale!"

Right On The Money

Does money bring happiness?

We end up with this: money doesn't make us happy on a day-to-day basis. We are, though, bombarded by messages telling us that we should value money and seek it out. So, like good members of society, we follow the convention.

What will make you feel happy right now? Acquiring money and status makes us feel satisfied with life. Through the "focusing illusion" we convince ourselves that satisfaction equals happiness. Unfortunately it doesn't. Even though we appear to have everything, we are left feeling that something is missing, but are unable to identify what that thing is.

That thing is simply this: feeling happy. Right now. In the moment.

What will make you feel happy right now?

Dean, Jeremy. "The 3 Reasons Money Brings Satisfaction But Not Happiness." Psyblog. Web, 15 May 2010 <http://www.spring.org. uk/2008/04/3-reasons-money-brings-satisfaction-but.php>.

Do you remember the thrill of getting the Sears catalogue in the fall—the "Wish Book"—Sears' special Christmas edition? Who hasn't seen children's eyes light up as they turn the pages of this magazine and dream of getting these magical new toys? Then parents are plagued with "I want..., I want..." from their children from September to December.

In our society of plenty there seems to be an unlimited number of things available to purchase—to make our lives easier, more comfortable, more fun, more productive, more enjoyable, and more, more, more! We don't believe we've ever met anyone who felt that they were making enough money or had so much money that they just couldn't spend it all.

Generally speaking—we're sure this doesn't apply to you or to us—members of our generation have developed a sense of entitlement. We feel that we deserve to have everything we want and if we can't have it then somehow we've been short-changed. In fact, we'll go so far as to say that quite often we equate the word *want* with the word *need*. How often have you used, or heard, the phrase, "I need that [or this or the other thing]" when what you really meant is "I *want* it"?

Remember those toys we were talking about, the ones that the children just had to have—life would be meaningless without them? They ached for it and we were convinced if we didn't get it for them their life would be ruined. How much time did we spend racing from store to store to find this "must have" item? How long did we wait in line to buy the toy that would bring a shout of joy on Christmas morning—remember *Tickle Me Elmos* and *Cabbage Patch* dolls? We wrapped it so carefully and then waited with anticipation to see the look on their faces when they opened that special package. Oh, yes, it was worth it! They were so happy and excited. And then to our disappointment, sometimes just days later, we saw that same toy that our child just "had to have" lying forgotten in the corner or even broken and useless.

We must often sound like children ourselves. We see something, hear about it, talk about it, wish for it, long for it and then finally buy it. Now we have cupboards, shelves and garages full of items that we *needed* too—unused and forgotten!

Social conditioning

We're bombarded with advertising every day. We're told what we need to eat, drink, wear, watch, listen to and own, and convinced that our lives will be less than they could be without these products. We've been persuaded that we need a particular brand or label; that a "no name" product doesn't taste as good as a brand name product or that the store brand jeans don't fit as well as the designer label. Sometimes that's true—mostly it's not. That's just what advertisers are paid to convince us.

How do we overcome this social conditioning?

Bill: Just a minute...I've been following you so far...but I'm not sure what you mean by social conditioning. It sounds like something that happens in a communist country...

Author: Wikipedia explains that social conditioning refers to the sociological phenomenological process of inheriting tradition and gradual cultural transmutation passed down through previous generations. ("Social Conditioning." <u>Wikipedia, The Free Encyclopedia</u>. Wikimedia Foundation, Inc. May 2007. Web, 15 May 2010 <http://en.wikipedia.org/wiki/Social_conditioning>.)

Bill: Huh?

Author: In simpler terms, social conditioning occurs when large groups of people begin to think, behave, dress, etc. in certain similar ways. For example, people who listen to the same type of music also tend to dress in a similar style of clothing. Another example is if everyone in your neighborhood owned a new car, you might feel some pressure to trade in your old clunker for a new car too —just so you fit in.

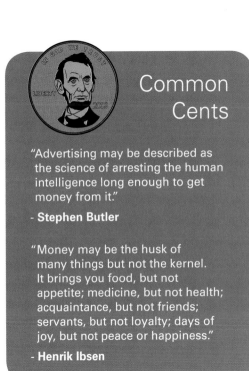

Common Cents

"Advertising may be described as the science of arresting the human intelligence long enough to get money from it."

- **Stephen Butler**

"Money may be the husk of many things but not the kernel. It brings you food, but not appetite; medicine, but not health; acquaintance, but not friends; servants, but not loyalty; days of joy, but not peace or happiness."

- **Henrik Ibsen**

It's possible to find lower priced substitutes for just about anything. It doesn't hurt to try something new or different and see for yourself. But we also need to decide for ourselves what is important—what are our priorities and goals and how can we achieve them. We can decide for ourselves and not be dictated to by societal pressures.

Living within your means

Now, if we want to get technical, and if we agree with Abraham Maslow (Maslow's hierarchy of needs), we can sum up our basic needs in a few categories—air, food, drink, shelter, warmth, and sleep. So we do *need* some things to survive physically—food, shelter and clothing—beyond that we are talking about *wants*. (Note the absence of a pick-up truck or big screen television under the category of basic needs.) To meet these basic physiological needs, we can grow, build or make these items or pay someone else for them. We can barter one thing or item for another thing or item or we can use money to purchase it. According to Webster's dictionary, money is used as "a medium of exchange and measure of value." Most of us exchange our time for money—a wage or salary. We exchange our money for goods and services—groceries, clothes, gas. It sounds simple doesn't it? The problems occur when our exchanges for goods and services exceed the amount of money we have. Ah—welcome debt!

There was a time when you couldn't spend more than you had. People saved for things they wanted to buy. The availability of credit changed that. Suddenly it was easy to "buy now and pay later." We were encouraged by stores to do just that. We've seen the consequence of living that philosophy recently. Today—after the 2007-2009 credit crisis—it's easier to believe that there are problems with the North American way of having it all—right now, whether we can afford it or not.

Maslow's hierarchy of needs

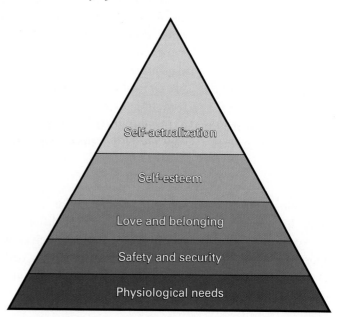

Your Money's Worth

Get free stuff! (when you buy other stuff)

These findings have been well-understood by advertising and marketing professionals for decades. Crowbarring the word *free* into any deal will usually improve its allure, even when, strictly speaking, you're not really getting anything for free.

Think about the ubiquitous "buy-one-get-one-free" deals in which you don't really get anything for free—you're just paying half the price. While half-price is good, it doesn't sound as good as free, does it?

Be aware of the seductive power that *free* holds over your mind—and you might decide you don't want to pay the price.

Dean, Jeremy. "Free! But At What Price?" Psyblog. Web, 15 May 2010 <http://www.spring.org.uk/2008/04/free-but-at-what-price.php>.

Many people mistakenly think that wealth is measured by how much we have or earn, disregarding what we owe. A big house, an expensive car, a backyard full of "toys" impresses us—but we don't see the balances on the mortgage, the car loan or the line of credit. We believe that wealthy people are people who make a lot of money. However, wealth is not measured by what you make or spend but by how much you *keep*.

The way to accumulate wealth is to consistently spend less than we make and to consistently put savings aside. When we pay down debt we will get to the point that we actually own our assets, and we increase our net worth: assets—what we own minus liabilities—what we owe.

Does that mean we should sacrifice everything today for something tomorrow? Of course not. We can't give up all present day pleasure for future comfort. It's true that we could save and save and give up everything for the future and die tomorrow. But perhaps it is just as foolhardy to live like there is no tomorrow and find that we don't die young (that's the downside?) and we've squandered all we had and left nothing for our future. Fortunately, there is a happy medium.

When we live within or below our means we create a financial buffer zone. What is our *means*?—for our purposes we'll define it as the income we have to live on after taxes are paid—our net income.

From our net income we pay our expenses. Our expenses include fixed items like mortgage/rent, car payments, insurance premiums, groceries and discretionary items like gym memberships, entertainment, and personal care. The remaining money can be saved or invested for the future.

If we are looking for more money, and we usually are, we can increase income, decrease expenses or do some combination of the two. More money doesn't necessarily solve the problem. People tend to spend what they make. If your income increases, but so does your spending, then you are no farther ahead. You need to make lifestyle changes for a lasting effect. You need to commit to putting money aside first, not only *if* there's any left over at the end of the month.

Fool's Gold

The Federal Reserve has released it's consumer credit report ending April, 2010. Outstanding consumer credit totals 2,440 billion dollars. This is made up of two parts, revolving credit (mainly credit card debt) which is at 838 billion dollars and non revolving credit (credit that can't be used again after it is paid off—student loans and automobile loans for example) which stands at 1,602 billion dollars.

"Consumer Credit." Federal Reserve Statistical Release. 7 June 2010. Board of Governors of the Federal Reserve System. Web, 30 June 2010 <http://www.federalreserve.gov/releases/g19/current/>.

Often we project onto money the power to fulfil our fantasies, calm our fears and ease our pain. We believe we can buy everything from hope to happiness and we become determined to buy the life we dream of. However, when we spend on credit we are buying this dream with someone else's money, and when the time comes to pay it back, these dreams can collapse.

Cottrell, Hazel. "The Psychology Of Debt." Credit Choices. A ConsumerChoices.co.uk website. Web, 15 May 2010 < http://www.creditchoices.co.uk/psychology-of-debt-help.html>.

In fact, we can employ a method used by many millionaires.... We can create an artifical environment of scarcity.

Penny: My turn...you know I'm going to ask! What's an artificial environment of scarcity?

Author: Artificial scarcity is an economic term describing the scarcity of items even though the technology and production capacity exists to create abundance. ("Artificial Scarcity." Wikipedia, The Free Encyclopedia. Wikimedia Foundation, Inc. 16 July 2010. Web, 19 July 2010 <http://en.wikipedia.org/wiki/Artificial_scarcity>.)

In the book, "The Millionaire Next Door," the authors reveal that many millionaires use this tactic to create wealth. "They create an artificial economic environment of scarcity for themselves and the other members of their household." (Stanley, T.J, and W.D. Danko (1996). *The Millionaire Next Door*. New York: Longstreet Press.) In other words, they act as though they had less to spend than they actually do. They invest their money first and then spend the balance—almost the exact opposite of what most of us do.

Maybe we could learn a lesson from someone who's net worth is $1,000,000 or more! If you are earning $50,000/year, but plan your budget based on a yearly income of $40,000, you have created your own artificial environment of scarcity. While more money is available to you, you act as though it is not, and save the difference. This marks the beginning of wealth creation.

You have the power to make changes in your life that will bring comfort and peace of mind. You're probably familiar with this saying, "The journey of 1,000 miles begins with a single step." (Economics and philosophy all on one page!) This book is about taking those first steps *and then* completing the journey. Don't worry, we'll be with you all the way!

Money Talks

Keeping up with the Joneses

[This] is a catchphrase in many parts of the English-speaking world referring to the comparison to one's neighbour as a benchmark for social caste or the accumulation of material goods. To fail to "keep up with the Joneses" is perceived as demonstrating socio-economic or cultural inferiority.

Origins

The phrase was popularized when a comic strip of the same name was created by cartoonist Arthur R. "Pop" Momand. The strip debuted in 1916 in the *New York World*, but strips appear in collections dated as early as April 1, 1913. The strip ran in American newspapers for 28 years, and was eventually adapted into books, films, and musical comedies. The *Joneses* of the title were neighbors of the strip's main characters, and were spoken of but never actually seen in person.

The philosophy of "keeping up with the Joneses" has widespread effects on society. According to this philosophy, conspicuous consumption occurs when people care about their standard of living in relation to their peers.

"Keeping Up With The Joneses." Wikipedia, the Free Encyclopedia. Wikimedia Foundation, Inc. 14 June 2010. Web, 30 June 2010 <http://en.wikipedia.org/wiki/Keeping_up_with_the_Joneses>.

We make these suggestions:

- Break societal norms. Change your focus from what society tells you is important to what actually *is* important.

- Remember that we *deserve* only what we can afford.

- Ask the question: Is it a true *need* or a *want* disguised as a need?

- Create your own artificial environment of scarcity.

- Provide yourself with a financial buffer zone.

- Find a balance—between present happiness and future comfort.

Did we just say you shouldn't have a big screen television or a pick-up truck? Of course we didn't—you can own things, as long as they don't own you!

If you take care of your needs first (we'll elaborate later)—and put something aside (we'll elaborate later)—and stay out of debt (again later), then you can take care of your wants and enjoy them guilt free. And if you get your big screen television, you can invite us over—we like movies, and we'll even spring for the popcorn and soda!

Let's move on...

Makes Cents

Are the things you're buying and doing adding value to your life?

Sometimes it pays (literally!) to stop and ask if the things we do and buy are adding value to our lives. If they aren't, why are we doing them? Often it's because things have become a habit. And as we all know, once things become a habit, they're pretty darn hard to change. They seem to slip into our subconscious and become a regular part of our lives.

That's great if habits develop for things like exercising daily and drinking plenty of water each day... But it's not so great if our habit is to pay the monthly cable bill without stopping to consider whether or not we even watch the channels we're paying for.

Other times we do things because it's the "expected" thing to do. Maybe society tells us we're "supposed" to buy a new car when we graduate from college or get a better job, but does a new car really add any value to our lives? It can actually do the opposite, if we go into debt or have to work in a job we dislike to pay for the car. It's good to keep in mind that we don't have to do the things that are "expected" if they aren't right for us.

Take a few moments and examine the things that you are buying and doing in your life. Are those things adding value? If not, what could you eliminate or change?

Used by permission from Jackie Beck.
Beck, Jackie. "Are The Things You're Buying And Doing Adding Value To Your Life?" Money Crush. Web, 23 July 2010 <http://www.moneycrush.com/adding-value/>.

Web sites used in the chapter

http://bit.ly/bl9HiI	(PSYBlog) "The 3 Reasons Money Brings Satisfaction But Not Happiness."
http://bit.ly/ctjPZk	(Wikipedia) A definition of "social conditioning."
http://bit.ly/aqyDki	(PSYBlog) "FREE! But At What Price?"
http://bit.ly/9oMsHl	(Federal Reserve) Consumer credit statistics.
http://bit.ly/b2yl24	(Credit Choices) "The Psychology Of Debt."
http://bit.ly/aMO2Cg	(Wikipedia) A definition of "artificial scarcity."
http://bit.ly/br9ugK	(Wikipedia) A definition of "keeping up with the Joneses."
http://bit.ly/aXNWXA	(MoneyCrush) "Are The Things You're Buying And Doing Adding Value To Your Life?"

Additional resources

Social conditioning

http://bit.ly/aOFHDv	(Personal Web Guide) A description of social conditioning and the affects of peer pressure.
http://bit.ly/9l0STL	(About.com) How using credit cards makes it feel like you aren't actually spending money.
http://bit.ly/bRcEs9	(HubPages) "Sales Techniques That Trick You Into Spending Too Much."

Living within your means

http://bit.ly/9oTc0H	(About.com) Explanation of Maslow's hierarchy of needs.
http://bit.ly/9Zudqf	(eHow) 14 steps to live within your means.
http://bit.ly/cnNHDM	(Ezine Articles) Article on unconscious spending and how to overcome it.

We asked, "What is your favorite story about money?" and you said…

Being part of a self-employed family has taught me to plan ahead. Sometimes the money comes flowing in and you just think it will continue in such abundance. You let your guard down and spend a little more freely than you might otherwise. Then suddenly, the money slows down and you can empty out your savings pretty quickly, just to pay the bills and get by. So I've learned to budget even when the money is good and just save it for the slow times, because they do come.

— **Nichola Wojnicz**

I like to say, "You can buy anything with $5.00 until you buy something." Your imagination runs wild, you can imagine yourself with all kinds of things, but if you delay the gratification and don't buy, it becomes something else….You will find that you get a great deal of pleasure by imagining what you can get even if you never actually get it…I am sure the thoughts alone release endorphins of pleasure...and you still have the $5. Try it. It is quite amazing.

— **Vickie Hartog**

We were trying to teach our children the value of just a penny. We took them shopping and told them that when they go shopping they need to ask themselves three questions: Do I want it? Do I need it? Can I afford it? They loved donuts. So one night they rolled all the pennies we had saved and then we found a donut store that would take some wrapped pennies for them! The children never forgot that just a penny can count.

— **Anonymous**

My grandfather always said that we should always work hard for our wages and never spend beyond our means.

— **Mary Goral**

My parents immigrated to Canada, each with only one suitcase. My father has always said that he wishes that I could make a better life for myself financially than he did. Now I look at my children and wish the same for them: financial intelligence. It's not about how much you have or don't have, it's how you manage it.

— **Kim Rybnikar**

My husband Glenn was approached by another company [with a job offer] when he was [already] working somewhere else. He went to the interview forewarning them that he was not a person who would be motivated by money as he was quite happy with his job but he was willing to listen to their proposal. When they offered him more than double his income he soon learned he could be motivated by money.

— **Valerie Davies**

Since having to participate in credit counseling (back in my 20's) due to not being responsible with credit cards, I've lived on cash for many years. I have a secured credit card now and I am repairing my credit one day at a time. I often ask myself when I want a big ticket item "Is this a need or a want?" If I reply "want"….I rethink how I want to pay for it.

— **Barbara Maxwell**

When my daughter was a little girl we were in a Chinese restaurant and they had a pond with Koi fish in it. You could throw pennies in the pond and make a wish, and she wanted to do it. She asked her dad for some pennies but he was busy talking to someone and ignored her so she decided to get them herself and put her hand in his pocket only to discover it wasn't her dad: surprise to her and the man. The lesson—always know whose hand is in your pocket.

— **Pam Hill**

One day my mother- and father-in-law had come home and they looked VERY guilty. SO guilty that we all had to ask what they had done. [They had eaten out at a restaurant.] The truth was that they had never gone out to eat at a restaurant until they were nearly 50. They said they couldn't afford to. They always paid cash for everything, INCLUDING their 3400 sq. ft. house and they worked at labor jobs making not much more than minimum wage.

— **Anonymous**

As newlyweds, one of our siblings shared this advice (which he learned from his Bishop): "If you are willing to live the first 10 years of your marriage like no one else would, you'll be able to live the rest of your marriage like no one else can."

— **Colin Fenton**

Chapter 2

Making Ends Meet

BUDGETING AND EMERGENCY PREPAREDNESS

"So…what do you think…do we pay our
electric bill or buy groceries this week?"

POWER SPENDING: Getting More For Less

Making ends meet...by ends, of course, we mean the end of your money and the end of the month. This seems to be a difficult concept to put into practice for a lot of people. Many people run out of money before they run out of month. This can start a downward spiral into a cycle of cash shortages and the use of credit to make up for the shortfalls. If you are in this group you *can* stop this cycle; if you take a close look at your finances, you can find a way to make ends meet.

If you're not in this group, good for you!! Ends meet and there's something leftover at the end of the month—excellent!! Please feel free to skip over to page 30; however, there may be something in these next few pages that you will find useful. Certainly it won't hurt to take a few minutes to find out.

One way to take a measure of your financial health is to put together a net worth statement.

Penny: Should I enroll in Accounting 101 or do I just need to hire a bookkeeper?

Author: It's not as intimidating as it sounds. A net worth statement provides a snapshot of your financial health. It can give a current financial baseline to measure future financial health. List your assets (anything you own: real estate, vehicles, investments, art and collectibles, etc.) and their value on one side of a page; on the other side, make a list of liabilities (anything you owe: mortgage, lines of credit, loans, and other debts) and the remaining balances. When you take the things you owe away from what you own, you are left with your net worth.

Penny: That's not so hard. I can do that.

Starting out in adult life, most people's net worth is low—zero or even less than zero—a negative net worth. This is to be expected. You have to start somewhere and sometimes the only way to go is up.

Money Talks

To make ends meet

Today [this phrase] often refers to money and having the ability to stretch your income to pay all your bills. The origin goes back to sailing ships with a lot of masts. Some were attached by ropes that moved. Some were hung by ropes that were permanent. When the lower ropes broke, the captain would tell the men to pull the ropes together, splice them to get the ends to meet again, pull and tug on the canvas so that the masts would be productive for sailing again.

Used by permission from Sheila Cicchi, at Brownielocks.com.

Cicchi, Sheila. "Who Came Up With That One?" Brownielocks. Web, 18 June 2010 <http://www.brownielocks.com/wordorigins.html>.

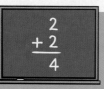

Do The Math

Net Worth = Assets - Liabilities

In fact, young people usually go through a stage of *dissavings*—a time when they go into debt for education, a vehicle or a home—a time before income catches up with expenses. But it is unwise to continue on this path.

From time to time, at least annually, you should recalculate your net worth and compare it to your baseline net worth statement. The goal is to move to a positive net worth—if you are not already there—and then begin to grow your net worth year by year. There are a few ways to make this happen. When assets grow and/or liabilities are reduced, net worth increases.

Use a budget

However, before you start worrying about assets and liabilities, you have to have an idea of your cash flow. For a really accurate picture, you need to find out what is coming into your household and what is going out. This is a time consuming task but there's really no way around it. Just a side note: If you're feeling a little anxious about starting this process it might be time to ask why. Maybe you've tried before and it just didn't work. Maybe you're afraid of feeling deprived. Maybe the dog ate your budget and you've never got around to making another one. We don't pretend to be experts who can figure out the reason for your budget phobias. We recommend that you face your fears, take a deep breath, square up your shoulders, and get to work. Anticipation is often worse than the actual event.

Even though it may be hard to start, today's efforts will reap tomorrow's rewards.

Although we won't go into great detail on creating a budget we will give you a brief overview of the *how-tos* of budgeting. (We have provided you with links on our website that will take you to worksheets that you can use to get started.) First, pull out your bank statements and credit card statements and see what's coming in and what's going out. That's the easy part; it's not hard to pick out those figures. These numbers should be transferred to your budget statement.

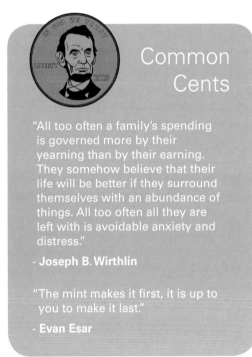

Common Cents

"All too often a family's spending is governed more by their yearning than by their earning. They somehow believe that their life will be better if they surround themselves with an abundance of things. All too often all they are left with is avoidable anxiety and distress."

- Joseph B. Wirthlin

"The mint makes it first, it is up to you to make it last."

- Evan Esar

Makes Cents

Living on a budget

One of the simplest but most powerful money making ideas is this: keep a daily log of everything you spend. Go to the dollar store and buy a little notebook and carry it with you wherever you go. Write down every penny—every single penny—you spend. It's as simple as that.

If you do this, you will find something magic happening in your financial life in just a few weeks.

There is something incredibly powerful about writing down all your expenditures. It makes the flow of money through your life more real and exact. It shows you simply and clearly just where you are spending your money, on what and why. Once you know that, it becomes much easier to control your spending.

Many people who have taken up this practice have not only learned something about themselves which they never knew before, but they are often astounded....The point is, it was their daily expense log that helped achieve the insight and clarity they needed to get control of their finances. That's what a simple spending record will do for you—it will give you control over your spending, and thus your financial life. There may be nothing but a 75-cent notebook and a ballpoint pen between your life of financial struggle and financial freedom.

Peterson, Palyn. "Tips For Living On A Budget." Debtsteps. Web, 15 May 2010 <http://www. debtsteps.com/living-on-a-budget.html>.

Probably a lot of those expenses are fixed expenses like mortgage or rent payments, property taxes, car payments and other loan payments, insurance premiums, etc. Fixed payments generally stay pretty consistent and can't be eliminated—at least until they are paid off.

However, variable payments change and are based on how many goods and services we use. This category includes groceries, car expenses, clothing and household utilities, and also entertainment, subscriptions and personal care. We might have more trouble figuring out how our money is spent in these categories. Though some of these payments may be made with automatic payments from a checking account, many of us tend to use debit, credit cards and cash for a lot of these variable expenses.

Grab a piece of paper and a pen and start writing down what you spend. A month's worth of tracking may be enough to give you a good picture of where the money is going. Keep in mind that some expenses don't come out every month. Then record these amounts on your budget sheet. (If you're just so excited to begin and don't think you can wait a month to get started, then estimate. Compare your estimates with the actual amounts at the end of the month and adjust your figures.) Grouping similar expenditures into categories (ie. groceries, dining out and ordering in can be grouped under Food) can help you to simplify your budget.

Once you've recorded what's coming in and what's going out, you can figure out if you need to make some adjustments so that your budget will balance. If expenses exceed income it's time to make changes. You can increase your income and/or decrease your expenses—does this sound familiar to you? It's a simple matter of math.

Now that you know what your income is, what your expenses are and how much you are planning to spend in each category, you need to keep track. How will you do that? Remember Bob Cratchet, the poor little clerk in Charles Dicken's story, "A Christmas Carol," writing figures in his ledger from dawn to dusk? My mother kept a ledger book and recorded her income and expenses, broken down into categories—everything in its neat little columns. Unfortunately, if there was a mistake there was a lot of erasing and recalculating to do.

Of course, we're not saying this method doesn't work—didn't we just tell you to write down all your *cash* purchases? Thankfully there are some other methods you might find easier and (hopefully) more enjoyable.

Some people determine their budget for variable expenses and then put the allotted cash into separate jars or envelopes, for each category. The expenditures can be recorded, for more accountability, on a piece of paper in each jar or envelope and the receipts can be stored in the container. This is the cash method of budgeting. When the cash is gone, the spending ends. Any money left over at the end of the month can be carried forward to the next month. From time to time, you must reevaluate the spending limits and reallocate funds as necessary.

If you are ready for a more technologically advanced method, you can track your expenses on a computer spreadsheet program, online or with a software program. You can set up your budget and then track your spending in each category to make sure you are staying on budget; you can anticipate future bill payments and paychecks, and download bank and credit card transactions.

If you are looking for a software program that's easy to understand and use, we have a suggestion for you!! Eric and Robin have created an online budgeting program, *Calendar***Budget**®, which lets you see daily account balances, and forecasts what will be in your account from day to day, month to month, and year to year based on your spending habits. You can see all income and expenses in an easy to view calendar format.

No matter which method you choose, it is best to record your expenditures weekly so that you can keep on top of your spending. Also, keep in mind that you will need to make adjustments to your budget from time to time—income and expenses will change. Set up a time to review your budget, perhaps monthly at first. Then, when you feel you have things under control, you can do semi-annual or annual reviews.

Your Money's Worth

Why should you use budgeting software?

1. It will help you to be organized.

2. Saves you time.

3. Helps to prevent mathematical mistakes.

4. Let's you see ahead.

5. Keeps you on track.

6. Helps you to set goals.

7. Gives you a sense of accomplishment when you reach your goals.

8. Puts you in control.

Using a budgeting tool that is effective, even if it costs a little, can end up saving you a lot of money. Find one you like and use it regularly to make sure that you stay on track.

Now you've planned and plotted, allocated and recorded, tried and tested your new budget. That's great, but nothing can derail a plan as quickly as an emergency or unanticipated expense.

Emergency planning

Let's address some of the BIG emergencies right away: illness, death and disability. These are risks that every individual faces. There is a way to manage that risk.

Bill: You mean besides checking my parachute before I jump out of a plane?

Author: That's a good idea. You should do what you can to stay safe but there are risks in living day-to-day that can't be avoided and in most cases you can manage those risks with insurance. There is whole life, universal life and term insurance. You can buy disability, accidental death and dismemberment, health, travel and life insurance. There is critical illness, long term care, home, auto, tenant's and mortgage insurance. Then you have to decide how much coverage you need and make sure that you understand what's covered under the policy.

Bill: There's so much to think about!

Author: Exactly, that's why we recommend that you speak to a certified financial planner or insurance specialist. A qualified agent can take you through an assessment process to make sure you are covered properly and adequately.

Though insurance issues are beyond the scope of this book, we feel it necessary to remind you of the importance of protecting yourself, your loved ones and your assets. It is imperative to protect current and future income and assets before beginning an investment program. This is one of the first steps when preparing a financial plan for individuals and families. After all, you *wouldn't* jump out of a plane without first ensuring all of your parachute straps and buckles are tightly fastened.

Factor This In

Why you need life insurance

The primary purpose of life insurance is to enable your family to continue their current lifestyle when and if you're no longer around. It is also designed to help meet specific needs that your family will have in the future.

Here are a few examples of how a good life insurance policy can protect your family:

- Life insurance will replace your lost income in the event that it goes away in the future.

- It can pay off your mortgage and provide your family with a debt-free home.

- Credit card and other consumer debts can be liquidated with life insurance benefits.

- An adequate life insurance policy will fund a quality education for your children.

- Final expenses can be paid from your life insurance proceeds, preventing the need for your spouse and/or children to have to deal with them at the worst possible time.

"Why You Need Life Insurance." RLROUSE. Web, 19 July 2010 <http://www.rlrouse.com/life-insurance.html>.

Since we are on the subject of topics that we are not actually going to cover in this book, we might as well recommend that you seek professional help to prepare your will and powers of attorney. These are legal documents that are designed to protect you, your family and your assets. If circumstances arise when you require a personal representative in matters of health care and finance, a power of attorney will give the necessary direction. After death, a valid will comes into effect. (And no, we are not recommending "do it yourself" kits, hence the advice to seek *professional* help.)

Enough of death, disease and disability! There are other emergencies that arise, hopefully not so dire, that can sidetrack a budget: like the car breaks down, the washing machine springs a leak, or the freezer goes on vacation. If you have something set aside to cover these emergencies, then you won't have to scramble around, taking money earmarked for other categories and sending your budget into a tailspin. With that in mind, you should start building an emergency fund. Make the payments that will build your emergency fund a part of your budget—you know, right after the insurance premiums!!

A big mistake that most of us make is to assume that when things are good they will stay that way. We don't foresee the possibility of change—a job loss, a reduction in income, an increase in expenses or a relationship breakdown—and so we spend as though we will always enjoy our current financial level. It is important to at least entertain the idea that our personal circumstances *could* change and then prepare as well as we can, just in case. This entails not just putting money aside but also getting an education and upgrading skills.

Start small, if necessary, but start. Something is better than nothing. Perhaps you could use the next income tax refund, or other windfall, to build up your fund. When do you have enough? Some experts recommend an amount equivalent to 3-6 months of your living expenses. Not only would this give you a cushion if there was a job loss, but would provide the means to take care of smaller emergencies. The money would have to be accessible and liquid but not so easy to get to that you are tempted to dip into it for anything other than emergencies. Personally, we don't know anyone with 3-6 months of net income sitting in an emergency fund. Certainly, it would take some time to accumulate that much money. Ultimately, you will have to decide what amount makes you feel comfortable and protected.

Right On The Money

Emergency funds

While two in three Americans say they have their credit card numbers, bank account numbers, and other financial information together in one place, only 51% say they have an "emergency fund" in case a disaster causes all their income to suddenly stop. Only about 4 in 10 Americans say they actually have cash on hand in case of an emergency. And only about 10% say they have $1,000 in cash available in case of an emergency.

Three in four consumers say they would use their savings account as a money source in case of an emergency. Fifty-six percent say they would use credit cards and 50% would borrow from a relative. Thirty-nine percent say they would use their 401k retirement account and 37% say they would use their home equity account.

Jacobe, Dennis. "Are Americans Financially Prepared For Disaster?" Gallup. October 18, 2005. Web, 15 May 2010 <http://www.gallup.com/poll/19264/americans-financially-prepared-disaster.aspx>.

It is possible to have other sources of emergency money available such as a line of credit or a borrowing account (or a rich relative). Whatever you decide, it should be set up before an emergency arises because, as Mark Twain so aptly pointed out, "A banker is a fellow who lends you his umbrella when the sun is shining, but wants it back the minute it begins to rain."

The final area of emergency planning that we would like to talk about is being prepared in case of natural disasters or if you are asked to evacuate. The following information is from the FEMA (Federal Emergency Management Agency) website:

- "Disasters disrupt hundreds of thousands of lives every year. Each disaster has lasting effects, both to people and property.

- If a disaster occurs in your community, local government and disaster-relief organizations will try to help you, but you need to be ready as well. Local responders may not be able to reach you immediately, or they may need to focus their efforts elsewhere.

- You should know how to respond to severe weather or any disaster that could occur in your area—hurricanes, earthquakes, extreme cold, flooding, or terrorism." (Are You Ready?" FEMA. 21 May 2009. U.S. Department of Homeland Security. Web, 15 May 2010 < http://www. fema.gov/areyouready/why_prepare.shtm>.)

Governments are urging their citizens to prepare 72 hour packs that would see them through an emergency until help could arrive. There are websites offering these kits for sale, or you could put together your own kit. Your budget could allow for an extra $10/week, for example, that could be used to purchase what you need for you and your family to survive for at least 3 days if there were no other resources available. A little cash on hand—in case the machines we rely on aren't working, a few emergency supplies—candles, flashlights, a hand-crank radio, and some food and water—can make an unpleasant time a little easier—or may even make the difference between life and death.

Bank On It

Are you ready?

Emergency planning and checklists

Prepare your family by creating a family disaster plan. You can begin this process by gathering family members and reviewing the information [on] hazards, warning systems, evacuation routes and community and other plans. Discuss with them what you would do if family members are not home when a warning is issued. Additionally, your family plan should address the following:

- escape routes

- family communications

- utility shut-off and safety

- insurance and vital records

- special needs

- caring for animals

- safety skills

"Are You Ready?" FEMA. 21 May 2009. U.S. Department of Homeland Security. Web, 15 May 2010 <http://www.fema.gov/areyouready/emergency_planning.shtm>.

We make these suggestions:

- Put together a net worth statement.

- Record, try and test your budget.

- Try out a budget software program—may we suggest *Calendar***Budget**® ?

- Make sure you have adequate insurance coverage in place.

- Create an emergency fund.

- Put together a 72 hour pack.

Fool's Gold

It takes more than money

- Mike Tyson earned more than 300 million dollars in his career as a professional boxer. Not enough apparently to keep him in the lifestyle he grew accustomed to—he filed for bankruptcy in 2003.

- Custody dispute court papers from 2007 show that pop singer Britney Spears is not in the money saving habit. Although she had a $737,000 monthly income, she didn't save or invest any of it. Some of her monthly expenditures included over $49,000 on two mortgages, over $100,000 for entertainment, gifts and vacations and $16,000 for clothes.

Yes, it takes more than *money* to make ends meet.

Okay, you followed our suggestions and now you know where you stand financially. You have a working budget in place and a system that allows you to track your income and monitor and modify your expenses. You have the insurance coverage you need to protect yourself, your family and your assets. You are preparing for the unexpected by starting an emergency fund and preparing a 72 hour pack.

Congratulations!! Now you're ready for the next step…

Web sites used in the chapter

http://bit.ly/9PKm2h	(Brownielocks.com) Origins of commonly spoken words, phrases and sayings.
http://bit.ly/arGdZq	(Debt Steps) "Tips For Living On A Budget."
http://bit.ly/dcQbw6	(RLRouse.com) "Why You Need Life Insurance."
http://bit.ly/df7TuO	(Gallup) "Are Americans Financially Prepared For Disaster?"
http://bit.ly/yn8ee	(FEMA) "Are You Ready?"
http://bit.ly/c4tn5t	(FEMA) "Emergency Planning And Checklists."

Additional resources

Use a budget

http://bit.ly/awYGy3	(CalendarBudget.com) Track and plan your income/expenses online using a calendar.
http://bit.ly/dp8W3G	(Mackenzie Financial) Net worth calculator from Mackenzie Financial.
http://bit.ly/dAG7vl	(About.com) A few things to consider if your budget isn't working for you.

Emergency planning

http://bit.ly/dm8597	(Ready.gov) You may need to survive on your own after an emergency. This resource will help you be prepared.
http://bit.ly/c7bunl	(GetPrepared.ca) Get your family prepared for an emergency.
http://bit.ly/busdxh	(About.com) "Why You Need An Emergency Fund."

We asked, "How have you prepared for, or coped with, emergencies?" and you said...

I cut back on frivolous spending and I also keep a savings account for such occasions.

— **Karen McAleese**

We tightened our belts, budgeted, asked family for help and borrowed money.

— **Timothy Holt**

Try to look at all the options—is there something I can be creative about—incur a small cost to repair something temporarily until I can cover the larger cost or find the money for it, put off a payment or divide up a payment for the expense over a period of time (sometimes it only takes asking the other party to work with you and they will).

— **Karen Bourne**

[We've done] very little short of having our wills and trusts in order. [My wife and I] have also discussed contingency plans in the event of a disaster.

— **Brad Garland**

We have excess money in the bank, food and supply storage for two months, and some fuel storage for home use. We keep our vehicles gassed up.

— **Hope Bailey**

We had a financial plan worked out from when we first had children. We discussed insurance coverage in depth, especially in case of disability. We continually educate ourselves on better ways to borrow and save money. We also have a financial planner, an accountant and a bookkeeper reviewing our finances.

— **John Wilson**

My husband and I have built up storage of many food and emergency supplies, as well as 72 hour kits for disaster evacuation purposes. Also, we have a secret stash of cash in case banks are not available or systems are down.

— **Donna Mazzei**

Everyone should strive for some form of self sufficiency, whether it's having a first aid kit in case of emergency, candles and flashlight in case of power loss, camping stove or BBQ to cook, and a stash of food and water. We have all the above.

— **Rick Poulin**

After the panic has left, the first thing I do is start rolling change. My sister and I have always saved change. It adds up fast and you don't even miss it. It has gotten us out of lots of unexpected expenses.

— **Kathy MacLeod-Barr**

We use our one credit card for emergency expenses when needed, but we hold off on purchasing anything else until our financial situation returns to normal.

— **Coleen DeBlois**

We have a line of credit as a back-up and if it has been needed we have made every effort to pay it back monthly in a timely fashion.

— **Linda Cormack**

Every month we commit to put at least $200/pay cheque, or $400/month minimum into our savings account.

— **Geoff Crane**

Valuable papers are put in a fireproof lockbox. We've given copies of wills and decision instructions in case of incapacitation to our lawyer and a family member. We have canned food and bottled water put aside for emergencies. Money is put aside in the house in case of emergency.

— **Anonymous**

We have always kept our debt under control in case of unplanned emergencies.

— **Michelle Ongena**

We have a garden and fruit trees and have canned and preserved our produce. We have water stored and 72 hour kits in backpacks in a closet. Our married children have copies of our important documents, pictures, etc.

— **Margaret Dansie**

We have food storage, probably enough for at least 6 months, plus everyday meal provisions for about 60 days. We also have a 72 hour emergency kit, ready to go in a duffle bag, including some sundries like toothbrushes and toothpaste, etc., which we revamp each 6 months (we restock and refurbish the perishables). We also have a significant amount of water stockpiled, probably enough for a week.

— **Amy Bowler**

P.S. A few comments "by the people."

Chapter 3
A Fool And His Money
CREDIT AND DEBT

"How much room is left on the Visa card?"

So far we've covered a little psychology, a little budgeting and a little emergency planning, but we're not ready to move on down the line to financial freedom quite yet. We only barely mentioned the subject of debt in the last chapter in reference to mortgages and loan payments. The truth is that America is a nation in debt. In fact, a recent article from the Associated Press reports that America's debt "stands today at a staggering $11.4 trillion—equivalent to about $37,000 for each and every American. And it's expanding by over $1 trillion a year." (Raum, Tom. "MOUNTAIN OF DEBT: Rising debt may be next crisis." News Tribune. 3 July 2009. Web, 3 July 2010 <http://www.newstribune.townnews.com/articles/2009/07/05/opinion/181op05debt.txt>.)

At the end of 2008, Americans' credit card debt reached $972.73 billion. Average credit card debt per household—regardless of whether they have a credit card or not—was $8,329 at the end of 2008. (Source: Nilson Report, April 2009) The average balance per open credit card—including both retail and bank cards—was $1,157 at the end of 2008. ("2009 Personal Credit Card Debt Trend And The Consequences." OnlinEarnings. Elva Lee. 14 June 2009. Web, 3 July 2010 <http://onlinearnings.com/2009/06/14/2009-personal-credit-card-debt-trend-and-the-consequences/>.)

With statistics like these it's imperative that we cover the subject of credit and debt in more detail. After all, we don't want to be weighed down by excess baggage as we try to move forward financially. Now, we're not pointing fingers or doing any name calling, but if the title of this chapter makes you squirm it's possible that it hits a little too close to home…

Avoiding debt

We suppose the best place to start this discussion is with the best advice we can offer. Keeping in mind that an ounce of prevention is worth a pound of cure, the ideal strategy would be to avoid debt in the first place. Use a savings account to save up for purchases; consult your budget before making purchasing decisions (yes, you really are supposed to stick to your budget once you've done all the work from Chapter 2); know your spending limits; use cash or debit cards; avoid pressure situations and impulse spending; don't use all the credit you have available; get pre-approved for loans and stay within the limits. Easy, right? Okay, not so easy. So, if we can't seem to avoid debt entirely, we will have to talk about making better choices about it.

Good debt versus bad debt

Few of us are able to save up and make large purchases with cash. Unless you are one of the clever ones who can, at some point you will probably have to go into debt. While ideally having no debt is where we all would like to be, some kinds of debt are better than others. Let's divide debt into two categories: good debt and bad debt.

Bill: Good debt, bad debt...how do I know the difference?

Author: Ask a few simple questions. Look at what you are purchasing...will the value go up over time—appreciate—or will it lose value—depreciate?

Bill: Okay, that makes sense.

Author: Does it get used up quickly or have lasting or long use? Can you deduct the cost of borrowing? How long will it take to pay off the debt? What are the risks?

Bill: Alright, I get it. It's not a straightforward answer. I assume you will explain it all in more detail?

Author: Of course...let's begin...

Let's talk about good debt first (always keeping in mind that the best debt is *no* debt and that this is our ultimate goal). It might make more sense if we give a specific example of a tangible asset—real estate. For many people, the goal of home ownership is still a top priority. If we had to wait until we could afford to pay cash for a home, we would be waiting a very long time. If we don't want to wait out the time by living in a tent in our parents' backyard, we will need to borrow money to buy a house and then make mortgage payments until the house is, in fact, ours.

What are some of the advantages of this course of action? We can move out of our parents' home and into our new home much sooner. This way everyone is much happier!! Financially speaking, homes usually appreciate in value over time. As we pay down principal, we increase our net worth. When we have to make regular payments over a fixed period of time, it becomes a forced savings plan. If that's not enough incentive, in some countries the interest on the mortgage is deductible at tax time, within certain limits.

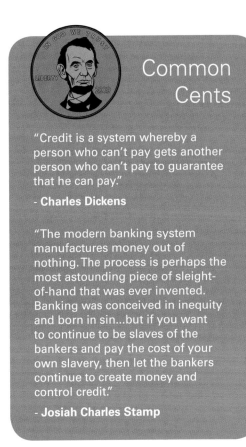

Common Cents

"Credit is a system whereby a person who can't pay gets another person who can't pay to guarantee that he can pay."

- Charles Dickens

"The modern banking system manufactures money out of nothing. The process is perhaps the most astounding piece of sleight-of-hand that was ever invented. Banking was conceived in inequity and born in sin...but if you want to continue to be slaves of the bankers and pay the cost of your own slavery, then let the bankers continue to create money and control credit."

- Josiah Charles Stamp

Fool's Gold

Public debt

It seems that many governments all over the world are not setting a very good example for the citizens of their countries when it comes to keeping their spending under control. The public debt statistics are sobering. Debt is shown as a percentage of GDP (Gross Domestic Product) for the year 2007.

Here's a list of the 10 "top" ranked countries:

Zimbabwe	218.2 % of GDP
Lebanon	186.6 % of GDP
Japan	170.0 % of GDP
Jamaica	126.5 % of GDP
Sudan	105.9 % of GDP
Egypt	105.8 % of GDP
Italy	104.0 % of GDP
Singapore	96.3 % of GDP
Seychelles	92.3 % of GDP
Greece	89.5 % of GDP

"Economy Statistics > Public Debt (Most Recent) By Country." Nationmaster. Web, 23 July 2010 <http://www.nationmaster.com/graph/eco_pub_deb-economy-public-debt>.

By the way, Canada comes in at #20 with 64.2% of GDP and the USA is ranked at #26 with 60.8% of GDP.

Just a note—while home ownership has been the best choice for many people, it is not without its dangers. As we witnessed in the latest recession, those who bought homes with no money down expecting that house prices would continue to rise were in a bad position when prices dropped and they had a larger mortgage on their home than their home was worth. In this case a *good* debt became a very bad debt and many people lost their homes.

There are other examples of good debt that aren't so tangible such as education, business and investment loans. The money is borrowed based on expectations of a higher future value on the money originally invested. The interest on these types of loans is often deductible as well.

Education is typically a good investment as it can increase future income. Statistically, the interest cost of borrowing to go to school will be dwarfed by the return (the higher wage earned from the resulting job/career) on your "investment." You will come out ahead, even after taking on some student debt. We will go into more detail in chapter 6 on the value of post-secondary education as it relates to future income.

Getting a loan for a business—starting your own or helping someone else—or for purchasing investments, can be a way to leverage the initial investment with a relatively smaller cost to yourself. You wouldn't invest unless you expected a good return. However, there is a risk that the business will fail or not meet the projected return; investments might not increase in value or could lose value. When money is leveraged both the return and the risk are magnified.

These loans provide an opportunity for growth on your original investment that is greater than the cost of borrowing but also increase your risk if the business or investment does not do as well as hoped. Use caution, get advice from trusted specialists and don't be taken in by "get rich quick" promises.

If what we purchase appreciates over time, if there are tax advantages, if there is future value—then we have *good* debt. What constitutes *bad* debt? The short answer is things we borrow for that don't meet the conditions described above (the even shorter answer is any debt, but we have to keep it real). Debt is considered bad when it is used to purchase items:

- that depreciate (electronics, for example)

- when the interest costs are non-deductible (personal items)

- when the interest rates are high (credit/store cards)

- when the item is used up before it is paid for (like restaurant meals)

- that are consumer goods (such as groceries or clothing)

- that you can't afford (you can provide your own examples)

- when the cost of the debt is higher than the return you are earning on your investment or savings

We want to elaborate on this last point as we seem to be contradicting ourselves. We advised you in Chapter 2 to include payments for an emergency fund in your budget. Does it make sense to keep money in a savings account that earns 1% when you have credit card debt that costs you 18%? Logically, of course it doesn't.

You *could* concentrate on paying off the debt and when it is paid off then use the debt repayment amount to fund your emergency fund. If you encounter an emergency along the way you will have freed up room on a credit card or your line of credit that you can use. Though the mathematics make better sense with this method, this could be dangerous as you may NEVER get out of the debt mindset and you may always be reaching for the credit card to fix things.

How about starting the emergency fund while paying down the debt? This will get you into a good habit and change your mindset in a positive way. You will be preparing, not fixing. When debts are repaid, then increase your savings.

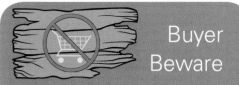

Buyer Beware

The *cost* of making minimum payments

My credit card statement recently changed and now includes a box detailing what it would cost me to pay back my balance under a couple different scenarios. The information highlights what a terrible idea it is to pay off the minimum balance on a credit card (or pay off the card in any way that takes a bit of time for that matter). Consider the following from a recent statement of mine:

- I had $2,888.74 in charges.

- If I made no additional charges on the card and only made the minimum payment ($28) each month, it would take me 18 years to pay off this debt and end up costing me $5,546.01.

- If I made no additional charges on the card and only made a payment of $95.36 each month (not sure how they came up with this amount—maybe it's the 36-month pay-off amount), it would take me 36 months to pay off this debt and end up costing me $3,432.96.

It's pretty clear from these numbers that making the minimum payment only is a very bad deal for the cardholder. I assume that's the point of the information—to make people see what a bad deal it is to hold on to credit card debt and to get them to pay it off ASAP.

My card has a 13.24% APR. The numbers would be much worse for a cardholder with a 15% or 20% APR.

"An Example Of Why Making The Minimum Payment On A Credit Card Is A Horrible Idea." Free Money Finance. Web, 3 July 2010 <http://www.freemoneyfinance.com/2010/04/an-example-of-why-making-the-minimum-payment-on-a-credit-card-is-a-horrible-idea.html>.

Is there such a thing as "good" *bad* debt? A vehicle loses value as soon as you drive it off the lot. However, a car is often a *necessary* bad debt, and one that can help you to boost your income—if it serves the purpose of providing transportation to a job or post-secondary schooling. Money spent to make money is generally a good investment providing it brings in more money than you would be paying out for the vehicle. However, having your own vehicle can be expensive. It's not just the initial cost; it's also the insurance, repairs and upkeep. Insurance rates and repair costs can vary greatly depending on the make and year of vehicle you choose, so research before you buy.

If there are other means available for getting you to where you need to go—such as walking, biking or public transportation, and owning a vehicle is more for your own convenience, then this item becomes a luxury. We're not saying you shouldn't have a vehicle. Perhaps a reliable secondhand vehicle will fill your needs and would be more affordable. You are more likely to be able to make a cash purchase in this case. In some instances, leasing may be a good option as well. In any case, vehicles usually depreciate in value—there are a FEW exceptions—so weigh all the options and make a decision based on what you need and what you can afford.

Use credit cards wisely

Again, some of the best advice about the use of credit cards is simply to not use them. However, many people like the convenience of using plastic. A credit card can be used as identification, it takes up a lot less room than a wallet full of cash, you will have a record of your purchases, and in most cases credit card companies provide free purchase protection.

Some people like to take advantage of the interest-free grace period (available on most cards) which is given to those who pay their monthly bills in full and on time. The prospect of reward points and free merchandise or travel, entices many people as well. If you use a credit card in this way, you should have no problem. Unfortunately, only about 40% of credit card holders pay off their balances monthly (credit card companies refer to these customers as *deadbeats*).

A prepaid credit card can be used like a regular credit card, but is paid in advance. Purchases are deducted from the card balance and it can be reloaded as needed. These cards offer the convenience and safety of a credit card but have a built-in spending limit—you can only spend the amount that you have prepaid.

Having just one credit card can make it easier to track, control and limit your spending. Avoid high interest cards that are offered by department and chain stores and don't be tempted by cards that offer low-introductory interest rates. Check the fine print for annual fees, late payment fees, and interest charges. If you decide to use a credit card, we recommend you find one that has no annual fee and a reward points system. Make sure you understand what you are signing up for when you agree to take a credit card.

How much debt is too much?

Penny: How do I know if I have too much debt?

Author: Check for these warning signs:

1. *Look in your savings account—if it's empty that spells trouble.*

2. *Are you only making minimum payments on your credit cards?*

3. *You have a wallet full of credit cards. You don't need more than 2 or 3.*

4. *You've reached the credit limit (on one or more) of your cards.*

5. *No one wants to lend you more money.*

6. *You are late making monthly payments.*

7. *You use a credit card to cover daily living expenses.*

8. *You borrow to pay the monthly payments.*

9. *Checks are bouncing.*

10. *You take cash or pay advances to get by.*

11. *You're not answering the phone...just in case.*

I think you get the idea. Even if a few of these ring a bell you should take a closer look and get things under control. You want to avoid the inevitable downhill slide—debt is a slippery slope...

Right On The Money

Personal debt

Although the U.S. economy and population are almost 10 times the size of Canada's, the two countries show several similarities. Both have relatively high per-capita income and living standards...Until the mid 1990s, both Canadians and Americans managed to spend less than their disposable income. However, from 1996 onwards, they spent almost all of it, leaving very little for saving...

Debt load, measured by the ratio of total debt to disposable income was almost the same for Canadians and Americans at the beginning of the 1980s. After that, they parted ways: Americans had the greater debt load between 1983 and 1991 and Canadians between 1992 and 2000. From 2001, debt grew steadily in both countries and by 2002 had surpassed disposable income. By 2005, for each dollar of disposable income, Canadians owed $1.16 and Americans $1.24.

The personal savings rate in Canada...peaked at 20.2% in Canada in 1982 and at 7.5% in the U.S. in 1981....By the late 1990s, however, the two rates were converging, reaching 1.2% in Canada and -0.4% in the U.S. in 2005.

"Perspectives On Labour And Income." Statistics Canada. January 2007. Web, 23 July 2010 <http://www.statcan.gc.ca/pub/75-001-x/commun/4096031-eng.htm>.

If you want to know what you can afford, as in what lenders *believe* you can afford, you can do a simple calculation. Lenders look at your debt-to-income ratio before considering if they will lend you money. This calculation is divided into two parts: the front and the back ratio.

"A debt-to-income ratio (often abbreviated DTI) is the percentage of a consumer's monthly gross income that goes toward paying debts. (Speaking precisely, DTIs often cover more than just debts; they can include certain taxes, fees, and insurance premiums as well. Nevertheless, the term is a set phrase that serves as a convenient, well-understood shorthand.) There are two main kinds of DTI, as discussed below.

The two main kinds of DTI are expressed as a pair using the notation x/y (for example, 28/36).

1. The first DTI, known as the front-end ratio, indicates the percentage of income that goes toward housing costs, which for renters is the rent amount and for homeowners is PITI (mortgage principal and interest, mortgage insurance premium [when applicable], hazard insurance premium, property taxes, and homeowners' association dues [when applicable]).

2. The second DTI, known as the back-end ratio, indicates the percentage of income that goes toward paying all recurring debt payments, including those covered by the first DTI, and other debts such as credit card payments, car loan payments, student loan payments, child support payments, alimony payments, and legal judgments." ("Debt-to-income Ratio." <u>Wikipedia, the Free Encyclopedia</u>. 1 June 2010. Web, 3 July 2010 <http://en.wikipedia.org/wiki/Debt-to-income_ratio>.)

Lenders will use this ratio to determine if you have too much debt and as a way to measure your financial well-being. They want to make sure that if they lend you money, you will be able to repay the debt.

However, just because a lender says that you qualify for a loan doesn't really mean that you can afford it or would be comfortable with the loan payments. Remember, they are in the business of lending money and earning interest. Their first interest may not be what's in *your* best interest. You must base your decision about what is affordable on your budget and stay within your comfort level. For example, when Robin and Eric bought their first home, they qualified for over $220,000, but set their own limit at $160,000 in order to keep their expenses modest and easy to maintain. This decision also allowed for changes in future income and expenses.

Do The Math

$$\begin{array}{r} 2 \\ + 2 \\ \hline 4 \end{array}$$

Debt-to-income ratio

There are three steps to calculating this ratio:

1. Add together everything you earn or receive each month.

2. Figure out what you spend on debt payments in a month. This includes mortgage payments—principal and interest, plus property taxes and mortgage and property insurance—your car payment, credit card minimum payments, student loan payments, child support/alimony payments and other monthly payment obligations.

3. Take the figure from #2 and divide it by the figure from #1, then multiply by 100 to figure out the percentage.

(This is the back-end ratio calculation.)

Getting rid of debt

If you find yourself with too much debt, what can you do? First, don't incur more debt. Stick to your budget!! Put your credit cards away and pay with debit cards or cash. Pay off the highest interest debt first and and the non tax-deductible loans before the tax-deductible ones.

We suggest you use a debt elimination calendar. Make higher payments on the most expensive loans, while making minimum payments on the rest of your loans. Once that debt is cleared, add the amount you were paying against it to the payment of the next highest interest loan. Continue to carry over the payment amounts from previous loans to the remaining loans as you pay each one off.

In many cases you can negotiate lower interest rates with your lenders. Make a few phone calls. Check our additional resources section on the website for some pointers.

If that's not enough, you may have to consolidate your loans. If you remortgage, this will probably extend your mortgage term and you will pay interest for a longer term; however, if it lowers the interest rate from a department store charge of 29% (or more) to 5%, that will give you interest relief and it will free up your cash flow. Don't make this a regular habit. Learn your lesson and change your lifestyle. There's no point in consolidating a loan and then repeating the same mistakes.

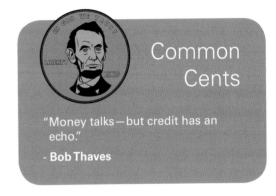

"Money talks—but credit has an echo."

- Bob Thaves

Debt elimination calendar

	Sears Card	Visa Card	Dentist	Piano Loan	Auto Loan
January	110	70	50	100	250
February	110	70	50	100	250
March		180	50	100	250
April		180	50	100	250
May			230	100	250
June			230	100	250
July				330	250
August				330	250
September					580
October					580
November					580
December					580

Need something more? There are organizations that can help if you feel it's too much to take care of on your own. Debtor's Anonymous introduces their program in these words on their website: "Debtors Anonymous is a fellowship of men and women who share their experience, strength and hope with each other that they may solve their common problem and help others to recover from compulsive debting.

Our primary purpose is to stop debting one day at a time and to help other compulsive debtors to stop incurring unsecured debt." ("Welcome To Debtor's Anonymous." Debtor's Anonymous. Web, 15 May 2010 <www.debtorsanonymous.org/>.)

What can you do about debt?

We feel that bankruptcy should be used as a last resort. We would like to remind you that there are alternatives to bankruptcy. Consider these suggestions from the Money Problems website:

- "Fix it on your own: decrease your expenses and increase your income.

- Consolidate all your debts into one debt with a lower interest rate. If you still have good credit, you may be able to borrow enough money, at a low interest rate, to repay all of your high interest debts.

- Work out a debt management plan through a credit counsellor. If you don't qualify for a debt consolidation loan, try a debt management plan through a credit counsellor.

- Negotiate with your creditors about paying a portion of the debt only. If you can't afford to repay your debts in full, your next option is a consumer proposal [if you live in Canada], or a Chapter 13 Wage Earner Plan [if you live in the United States].

- File bankruptcy and get a fresh start. If you can't afford to make even partial payments, your final option is personal bankruptcy." ("I've Got Debt: What Are My Options?" Money Problems. Web, 15 May 2010 <http://www.moneyproblems.ca/debt-management-options.htm>.)

There are local government and/or private agencies available to help you through your own personal credit crunch. Take advantage of the resources available and seek professional help. You don't have to go through this alone!

Makes Cents

5 reasons to STOP using credit cards

There are some pretty convincing reasons we should avoid using credit cards. Let's consider some of the dangers and pitfalls.

1. We spend more with credit cards.

2. Credit cards add debt to your life.

3. The risk outweighs the rewards.

4. Risk of late fees is reason number four.

5. One of the fastest growing crimes of today is identity theft.

Consider using a debit card instead. Debit cards work just like credit cards, offer the same protection if run through as credit cards, but don't add debt...Alternatively you can always pay with cash.

Zimmerman, Peter. "Five Reasons To STOP Using Credit Cards." CreditFactor. 2008. Web, 30 June 2010 <http://www.credit-factor.com/debtfree/stopusingcreditcards>.

We make these suggestions:

- Avoid debt whenever possible.

- Understand the difference between good and bad debt.

- If you use credit cards, use them wisely.

- Recognize if you have too much debt.

- Prepare a plan to get rid of debt—follow through with your plan.

- If it's too much for you to handle alone, then find help.

- Explore alternatives before you consider claiming bankruptcy.

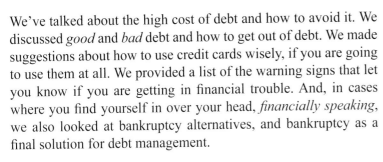

We've talked about the high cost of debt and how to avoid it. We discussed *good* and *bad* debt and how to get out of debt. We made suggestions about how to use credit cards wisely, if you are going to use them at all. We provided a list of the warning signs that let you know if you are getting in financial trouble. And, in cases where you find yourself in over your head, *financially speaking*, we also looked at bankruptcy alternatives, and bankruptcy as a final solution for debt management.

That was a pretty weighty subject and we hope we haven't loaded you down with too much information. The good news is that once debt repayment is in the process, we can finally move forward and think about putting something aside to meet our financial goals for the future…

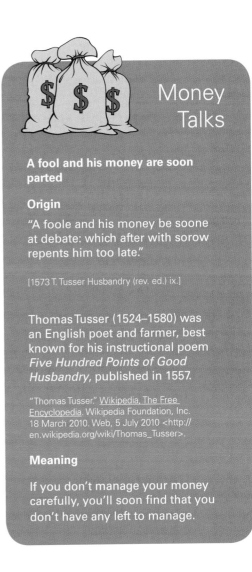

Money Talks

A fool and his money are soon parted

Origin

"A foole and his money be soone at debate: which after with sorow repents him too late."

[1573 T. Tusser Husbandry (rev. ed.) ix.]

Thomas Tusser (1524–1580) was an English poet and farmer, best known for his instructional poem *Five Hundred Points of Good Husbandry*, published in 1557.

"Thomas Tusser." Wikipedia, The Free Encyclopedia. Wikipedia Foundation, Inc. 18 March 2010. Web, 5 July 2010 <http://en.wikipedia.org/wiki/Thomas_Tusser>.

Meaning

If you don't manage your money carefully, you'll soon find that you don't have any left to manage.

Web sites used in the chapter

http://bit.ly/cGPvzS	(News Tribune) "MOUNTAIN OF DEBT: Rising Debt May Be Next Crisis."
http://bit.ly/9ntxST	(OnlinEarnings.com) "2009 Personal Credit Card Debt Trend and the Consequences."
http://bit.ly/97jPU9	(Productivity 501) "4 Reasons You Should Use a Credit Card."
http://bit.ly/Cnpsd	(Nation Master) Economy statistics.
http://bit.ly/ceVI3s	(Free Money Finance) "Why Making the Minimum Payment on a Credit Card is a Bad Idea."
http://bit.ly/9HJs0j	(Federal Reserve Board) "5 Tips: Getting the Most From Your Credit Card."
http://bit.ly/alGRpg	(Statistics Canada) Personal debt statistics for Canada and the U.S.A.
http://bit.ly/avPHJh	(Wikipedia) A definition of "debt-to-income ratio."
http://bit.ly/9JyxfM	(Debtors Anonymous) Stop debting.
http://bit.ly/9mPHJR	(MoneyProblems.ca) "What Can You Do About Your Debt?"
http://bit.ly/axVi0L	(CreditFactor.com) "Five Reasons to STOP Using Credit Cards."
http://bit.ly/cUxhu8	(Wikipedia) A brief bio of "Thomas Tusser."

Additional resources

Avoiding debt

http://bit.ly/asHaWt	(FindLaw.com) "Tips For Avoiding Debt."
http://bit.ly/cLHFiv	(About.com) "Five Spending Habits That Lead To Debt."
http://bit.ly/dltAyy	(PickTheBrain.com) "7 Tips For Avoiding A Lifetime Of Debt."

Good debt versus bad debt

http://bit.ly/9FO8SE	(MSN Money) The difference between good and bad debt.
http://bit.ly/bygrnl	(CNN Money) "Good Debt Vs. Bad Debt."
http://bit.ly/cpradx	(About.com) "Good Debt Vs. Bad Debt."

Use credit cards wisely

http://bit.ly/d5sUE7	(USA) (Annual Credit Report) Get your official credit report free annually.
http://bit.ly/dz75yb	(USA) (CreditOffers.com) Comparing rewards on credit cards.
http://bit.ly/deCtkh	(Canada) (RateSupermarket.ca) Compare all Canadian credit cards.

How much debt is too much?

http://bit.ly/9mvkjr	(MSN Money) "How Much Debt Is Too Much?" Online debt ratio calculator.
http://bit.ly/cKq2eR	(SmartMoney) "Do You Have Too Much Debt?"
http://bit.ly/az4Tfp	(About.com) "Managing Debt—Do You Have Too Much Debt?"

Getting rid of debt

http://bit.ly/aFcIqB	(DebtProofLiving.com) A simple approach to saving, giving and paying off debt.
http://bit.ly/99cWmx	(MSN Money) A "Consolidate Your Debt Time Frame" calculator.
http://bit.ly/aQ8fmJ	(BankRate.com) "10 Debt Consolidation Myths."

What can you do about debt?

http://bit.ly/9JyxfM	(Debtor's Anonymous) An organization that helps compulsive debtors.
http://bit.ly/clBEV7	(Bankruptcy Canada) "How A Consumer Proposal Works."
http://bit.ly/cWVWew	(GailVazOxlade.com) Articles and interactive worksheets regarding debt elimination.

We asked, "How do you handle, deal with or avoid debt?" and you said...

I now agree with my husband that we need to save up for an item before we purchase it. When I was single and didn't have any major debts, I had gotten into the bad habit of buying a few things on credit. It didn't get out of control, but it was really nice to get the things I wanted right away. When my husband and I got married, it was easy to see that we disagreed on our purchase strategy. My husband was (and still is) in the "don't buy on credit" camp. It took some time, but I can now see the value in living this way. There are always more things that I would like, but it is really nice to know that the things that we have are paid for. During our marriage we have purchased 2 vehicles without going into debt for them. These weren't new vehicles (that would be impressive), but they have been wise choices and have fit our family's needs perfectly.

— **Rachel Stoklosa**

I paid student loans off as slowly as possible. Mortgage is paid with regular payments plus 20%.

— **Chris McConnehey**

Don't make purchases that you can't pay for at the time. Credit cards and lines of credit should be used for convenience purposes and to use the applicable reward program that comes from that service. If you don't already have the money, don't spend what you don't have because whatever you're buying is not really yours and it will usually cost you a lot more in the long run.

— **Rusty Heffering**

Use bonuses and income tax returns to pay off any remaining debt at the end of year and make large payments until debt is gone.

— **Chris Wheeler**

Don't charge more than can be paid off with no interest.

— **Linda Austin**

Pay off the highest interest debt first by doubling monthly payments and/or making lump payments while making the minimum (or more if possible) payments on the lower interest debts.

— **Jenn Johnston**

Stay out of debt! When in debt, pay off the highest interest accruing things first.

— **Camille Brady**

Our best idea to avoid using credit was to save for [what we wanted to buy]. We've also sold an item in order to have what was needed: we owned a very special car my husband just loved, but we needed to renovate our bathroom so he had to make the painful choice of sitting on a new toilet, or being able to sit in his car. He chose the toilet.

— **Sandra Vos**

I have all of my debt on my LOC [line of credit]. I don't keep a balance anywhere else. I have my pay checks deposited to my LOC which ensures I keep my balance as low as possible. I don't use a checking account. So every time I take out money or use a debit transaction I remind myself—"This is debt you are taking out—and you are going to pay 6% interest on everything you buy—is it really worth it?" It also keeps me motivated since I can watch the balance go down faster!

— **Courtney Page**

We always use our tax return to pay debt down. We now only have a car loan and our home loan.

— **Matthew Brady**

We try to pay off any credit cards immediately. If we couldn't, we would pay down the ones with the highest interest first. When we had a mortgage, we did bi-weekly payments with the option of paying extra once a month. We went to a mortgage broker who happened to be our friend, and we always looked for a flexible pay down plan.

— **Patty Bush**

I use credit for all purchases and at the end of the month I have a record of what I spent....I get credit interest free for 26 days and then pay it off in full.

— **Shirlee Weeks**

Pay off highest interest [debt] first, before investing for lower gains.

— **Ryan Nickelchok**

Put any extra cash towards the debt to save on interest [costs].

— **Bonnie Brash**

We do our best to purchase with cash. When we cannot, we either wait until we can or we purchase with our line of credit.

— **Norman Johnston**

P.S. A few comments "by the people."

Chapter 4
A Penny Saved Is A Penny Earned
SAVINGS AND INVESTMENTS

"I think you're taking this energy savings
thing a little too far."

Now that we've made it through the first three chapters—money psychology, budgeting and debt—we can move forward at last. Let's look at this chapter's topic: savings and investments.

Goal setting

Though we all have many financial goals that we want to achieve, the time frame for achieving those goals can vary. Some of our goals are things we want in the short-term, others mid-term or long-term.

Some examples of short-term goals are saving for next year's vacation, or a new fridge. Things that you want to achieve in about 1 years' time.

Mid-term goals are achieved in 2-5 years' time. Maybe you are looking at making a larger purchase—a new car, a boat, or a down payment on a house.

Long-term goals are over 5 years away—your retirement, an inheritance for the children or even helping a child out with education, a wedding or a home purchase.

The first step is to decide what your goals are in each of these three time frames. It's not likely that you will be able to save for everything on your list, at least not right now. You will have to prioritize your goals in each area and save for the things that are most important to you. However, it's important that you don't neglect your long term goals in order to satisfy your short- and mid-term goals.

This is a good time to sit down with your family members to discuss what you want to achieve financially. If your spouse and children are part of the goal *setting* then they will be more likely to be a part of the goal *achieving*. You want everyone in your boat rowing in the same direction, otherwise, you'll find yourself going around and around in circles. When you have a goal in sight, it may not seem to be a sacrifice to give up something to achieve that goal. For example, children may be willing to give up the weekly restaurant meal in order to have a week at a cottage in the summer.

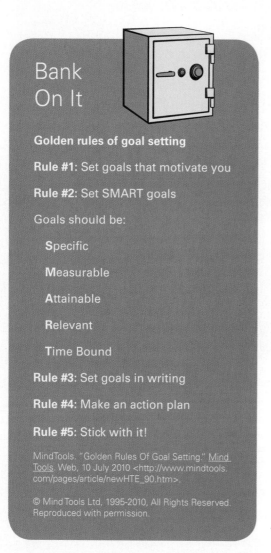

Bank On It

Golden rules of goal setting

Rule #1: Set goals that motivate you

Rule #2: Set SMART goals

Goals should be:

  Specific

  Measurable

  Attainable

  Relevant

  Time Bound

Rule #3: Set goals in writing

Rule #4: Make an action plan

Rule #5: Stick with it!

MindTools. "Golden Rules Of Goal Setting." Mind Tools. Web, 10 July 2010 <http://www.mindtools.com/pages/article/newHTE_90.htm>.

Weigh your options

For the sake of convenience, we will divide our goals into just two categories (short-term and long-term) as we discuss investment options. Since we are not actually offering any individual investment advice or recommending any particular investments, this will just be a general discussion to give you an idea about some of the different investment vehicles that are available. On our additional resources page at the end of the chapter we've included links to worksheets to help you with your investment planning. As previously mentioned, we advise you to seek the help of professionals. There are many products available and finding the right investments for *you* can be difficult.

It is essential that you choose appropriate investments for the money you put away to meet your short-term goals. Protecting your principal is a major concern since there is often not enough time for an investment to recover if there is a downturn in the markets. In fact, we'll use the term *savings* instead of *investments* to distinguish the shorter time frame.

The most obvious savings' vehicle for a short time frame is a savings or checking account—so the value of your original deposit will be safe (see the proviso below) though the interest rate is low. There are "high interest" accounts available now—often with no fees, no fixed terms and rates as high as with some locked-in products. These accounts are federally insured (there are conditions and limits) in most banks and saving institutions in the United States and Canada—look for the official FDIC or CDIC sign in the window.

There are some other options for your short-term savings including treasury bills, money market funds, and certificates of deposit. There are pros and cons to each one. Get educated, get some help, and remember—safety first.

Before investing for your long-term goals, there are several factors to consider: your income, your assets, your age, the time frame for your investment, your investment experience and your personal comfort level.

Right On The Money

Short term savings products

Treasury bills "[These are] a negotiable debt obligation issued by the...government and backed by its full faith and credit, having a maturity of one year or less...also called Bill or T-Bill."

"Treasury Bills." Investor Words. WebFinance Inc. Web, 5 July 2010 <http://www.investorwords.com/5060/Treasury_Bill.html>.

Money market funds "These funds invest in short term (one day to one year) debt obligations such as Treasury bills, certificates of deposit, and commercial paper. The main goal is the preservation of principal, accompanied by modest dividends."

"Money Market Funds." Investor Words. WebFinance Inc. Web, 5 July 2010 <http://www.investorwords.com/3107/money_market_fund.html>.

Certificates of deposit "Short- or medium-term, interest-bearing, [government] insured debt instrument offered by banks and savings and loans. CDs offer higher rates of return than most comparable investments, in exchange for tying up invested money for the duration of the certificate's maturity. Money removed before maturity is subject to a penalty. CDs are low risk, low return investments, and are also known as "time deposits," because the account holder has agreed to keep the money in the account for a specified amount of time, anywhere from three months to six years."

"Certificate Of Deposit." Investor Words. WebFinance Inc. Web, 5 July 2010 <http://www.investorwords.com/808/Certificate_of_Deposit.html>.

Let's talk about risk

This is probably a good time to talk about risk. Every investment has risk—even "guaranteed" products. For example, the guarantee on a guaranteed investment is only as good as the financial institution that backs it—this is a *financial* or *credit* risk. There are a few other types of investment risks that we'll briefly mention here. (Again, for a more in-depth look at this topic go to our additional resources page at the end of the chapter.) *Capital risk* is the risk that you might lose some or all of your investment—your capital. *Inflation risk* is the risk that your investment return will not keep pace with the inflation rate, resulting in a decrease in purchasing power. *Liquidity risk* describes the risk that you may not be able to sell your investment when you want to. You may incur a loss, or may not be able to take a gain. It's possible that you may not be able to sell at all or only a portion of your investment.

Okay, stay away from that mattress. While we felt we should mention risk, we don't want to scare you away from saving and investing. After all, there is a much bigger risk...not having anything at all. You can reduce risk by diversifying your portfolio. Diversification is a strategy that uses a variety of investments in a portfolio. Risk is reduced as investments are not concentrated in one type of investment so fluctuations in one sector will have less impact on the portfolio as a whole. In other words, when you diversify your portfolio you don't put all your eggs in one basket.

A risk tolerance assessment which is based on your own particular situation will help to determine the appropriate asset allocation for your investments. Asset allocation is the mixture of cash (income products), stocks and bonds in your portfolio. Asset allocation can reduce the risks of investing, but keep in mind that there is no simple formula that can determine the perfect asset allocation for every investor. However, there seems to be a consensus among financial services professionals that the asset allocation of a portfolio is the single most important factor in determining the return on your investments. How you allocate your investments between stocks, bonds and cash (and cash equivalents) is more important than the individual securities selection you make.

Common Cents

"In the old days a man who saved money was a miser; nowadays he's a wonder."

- **Unknown**

"Those who understand compound interest are destined to collect it. Those who don't are doomed to pay it."

- **Anonymous**

"The safest way to double your money is to fold it over and put it in your pocket."

- **Kin Hubbard**

Be sure to check with your bank or financial institution to see if there are charges or fees, minimum balances required or penalties for early withdrawals on any of the savings or investment choices you make, *before* you invest your money.

Some individuals may decide to choose other appreciating assets for their long term investing. Non-traditional investments include things like real estate, art, antiques, coins, and other collectibles. They are not without their risks as well. The value of these assets is often determined by supply and demand and public opinion—for example, art. You can also face liquidity risk if there is no interested buyer when you want to sell. A good example of some of the costs and risks can be illustrated in one non-traditional investment asset: real estate.

When you purchase a rental property, for example, you expect that you will have someone renting the property and making regular monthly payments that will cover the costs of owning the property. However, houses do require regular upkeep and maintenance and repair costs may be higher than expected. If a problem comes up and you can't do the work yourself—the furnace breaks down or the plumbing backs up—you will have to pay someone else to do the work.

You also have to find and keep renters and you risk going through periods of time with no tenants and no income. A worse situation may be bad tenants. Sometimes tenants don't or won't pay, and may even damage the property. Then it can be a nightmare to get them out of the house.

If circumstances arise when you want or need to sell the property you may not be able to find a buyer right away or may not be able to get the price you want. You may have to sell at a loss or you may not be able to sell at all. In this case you may find yourself in a financial bind, and perhaps may even lose the property.

What's our point? Just this: there are costs and risks associated with non-traditional investments that should also be considered before you make a purchase.

Your Money's Worth

Tips to save energy today

[Here are] easy low-cost and no-cost ways to save energy.

- Install a programmable thermostat to keep your house comfortably warm in the winter and comfortably cool in the summer.

- Use compact fluorescent light bulbs with the ENERGY STAR® label.

- Air dry dishes instead of using your dishwasher's drying cycle.

- Turn off your computer and monitor when not in use.

- Plug home electronics, such as TVs and DVD players, into power strips; turn the power strips off when the equipment is not in use (TVs and DVDs in standby mode still use several watts of power).

- Lower the thermostat on your hot water heater to 120°F [49°C].

- Take short showers instead of baths.

- Wash only full loads of dishes and clothes.

- Drive sensibly. Aggressive driving (speeding, rapid acceleration and braking) wastes gasoline.

- Look for the ENERGY STAR® label on home appliances and products. ENERGY STAR® products meet strict efficiency guidelines set by the U.S. Department of Energy and the Environmental Protection Agency.

"Tips To Save Energy Today." Energy Efficiency and Renewable Energy. 22 January 2009. U.S. Department of Energy. Web, 5 July 2010 <http://www1.eere.energy.gov/consumer/tips/save_energy.html>.

Setting money aside

A common question is "How much should I save?" There's no quick and easy answer or "one size fits all" dollar amount. There are so many things to think about. Short-term saving and long-term investing goals have to be decided on, and prioritized, as we mentioned before.

The general rule of thumb is that you will need about 70% of your pre-retirement income to live comfortably during your retirement years. But when you think about your retirement you have to answer several questions: What are you planning to do during retirement—sit on the porch in a rocking chair or travel the world? Will you be entitled to government benefits? Do you have an employer pension plan or do you have to fund your retirement all by yourself? Are you planning to leave an inheritance for the kids or do you want to spend all your money yourself? The answers to these questions will determine how much you need to save.

Again, the standard advice seems to be that you should save 10% of your income, but others have suggested up to 15% to 20%. I overheard a woman who said that her family lived on 50% of their household income. I wanted to ask if they made a phenomenal amount of money but practiced great restraint and discipline or if they just practiced great restraint and discipline and went without a lot of things. Certainly, it won't be a big adjustment or hardship for that family to move from their working income to their retirement income when they are already accustomed to living on only 50% of their income.

But let's get back to reality. The personal savings rate in 2006 (as a percentage of disposable income) was -1%, the lowest in 73 years. (Source: U.S. Department of Commerce) Since the credit crisis, it has been rising but is still a far cry from 10%, let alone 20% or 50% of income. But you have to start somewhere, and a financial plan can help you to sort out the amounts you need to save, based on your unique situation and on your own personal goals (short-, mid- and long-term). This plan will give you direction. Our advice is to start!

Finding the money

Once you have your plan in mind, you will have to find the money to fund it.

Penny: *That's the problem isn't it? Where will I find money to save?*

Author: Here's a few ideas to get you on your way, some **techniques** *for saving:*

- *Put money aside at the beginning of the month.*

- *Set up an automatic payment from your account.*

- *Overestimate expenses and underestimate your income—save the difference.*

- *Play "beat the budget" and when you spend less than the projected amount, put it aside.*

- *If you are an employee have your tax reduced at source to avoid a refund at tax time and put the increase in your pay check into a savings account.*

- *When a debt is paid off, use the payment to increase your savings.*

- *Get a part-time job.*

- *Make extra money from a hobby to save to meet a specific goal.*

When you start to put money aside, you want to be careful not to *commingle* your savings with your other money. It will be much easier to spend your savings if all your money is in one pot. It's also harder to see the savings add up when everything is all lumped together. Consider a separate account for your savings, one that will earn you a little extra and that isn't too easy to tap into. You'll have the satisfaction of seeing your balance grow month by month and then enjoy the rewards of meeting the financial goals that you have set.

Makes Cents

Spending your money wisely

Spending money is easy. Spending money wisely is another thing altogether....Remember to:

- **Shop around.** A "sale" price isn't always the "best" price. Some merchants may offer a sale price on the item you want for a limited time; other merchants may offer items at a discount everyday. Other merchants may offer a deep discount on one item—but only if you agree to spend a minimum that is several hundred dollars more.

- **Go online.** Check out websites that compare prices. If you decide to buy from an online merchant, keep shipping costs and delivery time in mind.

- **Look for price matching policies.** Some merchants will match, or even beat, a competitor's prices.

- **Clip coupons.** Coupons are useful when they save you money on what you're already planning to buy.

- **Use debit and credit cards sparingly.** Try to limit credit card purchases to an amount you can pay in full at the end of the month. If you use a debit card, don't rely on an overdraft feature to spend money you don't have....

- **Keep track of your spending.** Jotting down what you spend after every purchase helps keep you mindful of your limits.

Adapted from: "Money Matters: Spending." Federal Trade Commission. Federal government. Web, 23 July 2010 <http://www.ftc.gov/bcp/edu/microsites/moneymatters/managing-your-spending.shtml>.

Rule of 72

Time also can be your friend. Let's talk about the rule of 72.

Do The Math

2
+ 2
4

Rule of 72

At 3%		At 6%		At 12%	
Money doubles every 24 years		Money doubles every 12 years		Money doubles every 6 years	
Age	Value	Age	Value	Age	Value
18	$1000	18	$1000	18	$1000
42	$2000	30	$2000	24	$2000
66	$4000	42	$4000	30	$4000
		54	$8000	36	$8000
		66	$16000	42	$16000
				48	$32000
				54	$64000
				60	$128000
				66	$256000

We used these annual rates of return simply because they made it easy to do the chart in the most impressive way. We're not implying that you should find an investment that would earn 12% on an annual basis—we just wanted to illustrate the Rule of 72 in (theoretical) action. Past performance of any investment does not guarantee future performance and generally speaking the higher the investment return potential, the greater the risk.

Bill: Let me guess…by the time you reach the age of 72 you'll have enough money to retire?

Author: Not quite…it actually has nothing to do with your age.

The "Rule of 72" is a simplified calculation to help an investor understand how long it would take a sum of money to double at any given fixed annual rate of return. If you divide 72 by the annual rate of return, the result is an estimate of the number of years it would take for your investment to double in value. For dramatic effect, let's go through a couple of scenarios. A dollar invested at 2% would grow to $2 in about 36 years. That same dollar earning 12% would double in about 6 years. At the end of the 36 year time period, it would have grown to about $12.

(Note, I'm choosing annual rates of return based on ease of calculation only and taxes, which may or may not be payable, have not been factored into the calculation.)

Bill: Let's see…I have some of my retirement savings in an account that is paying me about 6%. So, 72/6 =12…it will take about 12 years for my money to double?

Author: I think you've got it!

The rule of 72 illustrates the beauty of compound interest— earning interest on your interest. As we've said, time is your friend when compound interest is working for you and not against you. In fact the earlier you start to invest the better. We've seen a chart that illustrated the advantage of early investing. It compared two investors who wanted to retire at the same age and wanted to accumulate the same amount of money; however, because the second investor didn't start to invest until 10 years after the first investor, he had to contribute more than double the amount to end up in the same (financial) place. To summarize the lesson learned from this example into a single sentence: *When investing, the sooner the better*.

Do I have to do this alone?

Many citizens qualify for at least some government benefits during their retirement. The government does provide statements that give you the amount of your personal entitlement. Usually at least a portion of this benefit is based on your contributions made to the program during employment years. It is important to remember that these social security plans were never intended to provide your entire retirement income but only to give you a base to build on.

Fortunately, there are incentives from employers and the government to help you save. There are pension plans that are intended to provide an income during retirement. These plans are tax-sheltered (investment income is not taxed while in the plan) and some or all of the income is tax-deferred (the money contributed is not taxed until later). In a tax-sheltered and tax-deferred plan, your investment is able to compound without taking a tax hit while it is being built up, and you won't pay taxes on it until it is withdrawn, hopefully during retirement.

If your company has a pension plan your employer will be able to give you more detailed information on your particular plan.

Factor This In

Top 10 ways to prepare for retirement

- Know your retirement needs.

- Find out about your social security benefits.

- Learn about your employer's pension or profit sharing plan.

- Contribute to a tax-sheltered savings plan.

- Ask your employer to start a plan.

- Don't touch your savings.

- Start now, set goals, and stick to them.

- Start early.

- Consider basic investment principles.

- Ask questions.

Financial security doesn't just happen. It takes planning and commitment and, yes, money.

"Top 10 Ways To Prepare For Retirement." Department of Labor. United States Government. Web, 23 July 2010 <http://www.dol.gov/ebsa/ Publications/10_ways_to_prepare.html>.

We'll just briefly discuss two different types of pension plans: defined benefit and defined contribution. The first type is going the way of the dodo bird—it's facing extinction. These plans provide a guaranteed retirement income that is based on a formula (income, years worked and the age at retirement) and not on the investment return. The company takes the risk that they will have to make up the difference between what has accumulated in the pension fund and what has to be paid out.

In a defined contribution plan, the contributions are known—and invested—but the future payout will depend on how well the investment does (or does not) before retirement. The individual bears the risk, but also hopefully enjoys the rewards. This is the most common form of retirement plan today.

Some retirement plans are totally funded by the individual and some employee pension funds have employer matching (up to a certain percentage of salary that is contributed). There are even plans that are funded entirely by the employer but these types of plans are few and far between and if you are part of one, you already know it! (Hey Canadians, take a look in our additional resources for information on the new tax-free savings account— no tax on investment income EVER.)

Employees are encouraged to speak to their employer to find out what is available. There are also many government websites and information centers to answer any questions you may have about government retirement benefits and retirement savings programs.

Also, there are education savings programs available to help fund education, if that is one of your goals, and other tax incentives to help students. We will cover these in chapter 6.

Now that you have some information on savings and investments, you can start to save for the future and enjoy all the rewards that will come with it!

Fool's Gold

Bigness bias

"Bigness bias" [The] tendency to discount the importance of numbers that represent a small percentage of a bigger purchase.

"John T. Reed's review of Belsky and Gilovich's book *Why Smart People Make Big Money Mistakes*." John T Reed. November 1998. Web, 15 May 2010 <http://www.johntreed.com/review_why_smart_people_make_big_money_mistakes.html>.

When negotiating your house price, you may be willing to spend an extra $500 on a minor upgrade on a $220,000 house without much worry, but you care enough to travel across the city to save a few dollars on your groceries. Extra charges look smaller when they are wrapped into big purchases; $500 is still $500 even though it's buried in a larger amount.

We make these suggestions:

- Set short-, mid- and long-term financial goals.

- Weigh your options—financially speaking.

- Make an investment plan.

- *Find* money for savings/investments.

- Understand how to put time on your side.

- Take advantage of government and employer incentives.

- Start to save. Now!

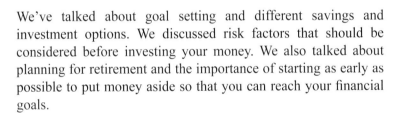

We've talked about goal setting and different savings and investment options. We discussed risk factors that should be considered before investing your money. We also talked about planning for retirement and the importance of starting as early as possible to put money aside so that you can reach your financial goals.

Are you fired up and ready to go? It's a good feeling isn't it? Since you are starting *now* to save for specific goals, let's look at how you can spend your money better, once you have it to spend...

Money Talks

A penny saved is a penny earned

Origin

Although the exact origin is unknown, it appears that this phrase is often incorrectly attributed to Benjamin Franklin. He did use the phrase, "A penny saved is twopence clear," in his *Poor Richard's Almanack* publication. However, there have been many variations of this phrase used over the last 350+ years.

Meaning

If you don't spend your penny you still have it. The penny that is saved is actually "earned" because it is still in your hand at the end of the day. If you find a penny, it's similar to earning it. A penny saved can earn more money when it is invested.

You get the idea...the less you spend, the more you keep. And as we've said before, the measure of wealth is not in the amount you earn but in the amount you keep!

Web sites used in the chapter

http://bit.ly/K887P	(Mind Tools) "Golden Rules Of Goal Setting."
http://bit.ly/9bsGaT	(InvestorWords.com) A definition of "Treasury Bill."
http://bit.ly/ba6Ivn	(InvestorWords.com) A definition of "Money Market Fund."
http://bit.ly/aUp3Y0	(InvestorWords.com) A definition of "Certificate of Deposit."
http://bit.ly/ajCFMj	(US Dept of Energy) "Tips To Save Energy Today."
http://bit.ly/9UWjqL	(BillShrink.com) "The Collapse Of Personal Savings Rate In America."
http://bit.ly/c3nktg	(Federal Trade Commission) "Spending Money Wisely."
http://bit.ly/cazlfm	(United States Department of Labor) "Top 10 Ways To Prepare For Retirement."
http://bit.ly/broYYB	(JohnTReed.com) "Why Smart People Make Big Money Mistakes."

Additional resources

Goal setting

http://bit.ly/cLYt7u	(Rutgers.edu) Financial goal setting worksheet.
http://bit.ly/9VfELA	(utk.edu) "Setting & Achieving Financial Goals."
http://bit.ly/dmxUqc	(About-Goal-Setting.com) "Financial Goal Setting—4 Steps."

Weigh your options

http://bit.ly/biGXeW	(CFP.net) Learn about Certified Financial Planners.
http://bit.ly/9T6M69	(Investor.gov) Government information site for investors.
http://bit.ly/anG5pW	(GetSmarterAboutMoney.ca) Money and investing information.

Let's talk about risk

http://bit.ly/dmDoNK	(RiskProfiling.com). Helping people make better financial decisions.
http://bit.ly/c9a5Ci	(PortfolioMonkey) Risk and return estimates for stocks, mutual funds and ETF's.
http://bit.ly/bKOIuf	(MSN Money) Risk tolerance quiz.

Setting money aside

http://bit.ly/9qivTC	(ChooseToSave.org) Retirement needs calculator.
http://bit.ly/auC4LQ	(CNN Money) Money calculators.
http://bit.ly/bVuTDC	(Yahoo Finance) Retirement calculators and how-to guides.

Finding the money

http://bit.ly/cN2ggz	(SavingsNut.com) Save money with minimal lifestyle changes.
http://bit.ly/bligp1	(GoodHousekeeping.com) 50 cutbacks you'll barely notice.
http://bit.ly/axKeWT	(PowerWise.ca) How to conserve energy at home.

Rule of 72

http://bit.ly/bHnbyq	(MoneyChimp.com) Rule of 72 calculator.
http://bit.ly/92tOgB	(MacKenzie Financial) Investing early calculator.
http://bit.ly/9ugyqv	(BetterExplained.com) "The Rule Of 72."

Do I have to do this alone?

http://bit.ly/bIcb1U	(USA) (Social Security) "Plan Your Retirement."
http://bit.ly/9wSD6g	(USA) (Social Security) Benefit online estimator and application.
http://bit.ly/af0g47	(Canada) (Services Canada) Old Age Security (OAS) Program.

We asked, "What strategies do you use to save for a future purchase or retirement?" and you said...

We save bonuses, holiday pay, etc.

— **Mike Chisholm**

I pay myself first—into a separate bank account. I try to ease back on grocery spending.

— **Veronica Albers**

I saved my $1 and $2 coins to buy a dishwasher and walked into the store with my coins and paid for it.

— **Tammy Terry**

We work overtime and have some of it paid out to us and use it to purchase expensive items. Also, we put money into our savings and use it when it reaches the amount we need.

— **Caitlin Blazina**

My wife Cathie had secretly saved $1000 from her house money and surprised me when we went on vacation.

— **Michael Norwick**

I chose to retire early but I planned (and prepared) to get another job after retiring, to supplement my pension income.

— **G. S.**

For the most part our main residence has been our retirement plan. To that end, we have had to be very careful in our house purchases, picking houses in areas and cities that we could reasonably expect to see significant appreciation in value. We have been lucky in that respect, with our first house doubling in value in 18 months, and then our present house almost quadrupled in value over a period of 22 years. We believe that the trick is to...down-size our residence [before the rest of the baby boomers do].

— **Anne Hindley**

We have bought a business and, hopefully, it will pay dividends when we retire. We also buy retirement savings products.

— **Hugh Coutts**

We have been doing better at saving money and then going out to shop. It's more fun that way to know you have up to $500, for example, to spend on a day out to stock up and get what you need without going into debt on basics. You can have a lot of fun shopping and quite often I find that I don't use all of the money set aside.

— **Carol Lancaster**

We like to rent a cottage each year for a week. This will be our 5th year. We take the whole family, kids, grandkids and dogs. In-laws can visit for a day or two. It's our gift to the family. (It's actually for us—don't tell them.) It's a blessing having them all under one roof again, even if for a short time. It's always been hard for us to save—growing family and all...but having a short-term goal annually has made it possible for us to see that it happens. It's made longer-term saving a reality.

— **Lynn Yates**

I'm building ownership in businesses that will generate perpetual income [for my retirement years].

— **Stephen Palmer**

We contribute monthly to retirement savings plans and have a forced savings account that we contribute to monthly as well. We budget our money and try not to spend frivolously.

— **Ian Cormack**

I wish I was [saving for retirement...I'm] looking for large inheritances.

— **C. T.**

Through my employee share plan where the company matched 40% of my contribution every pay period, we were able to pay for our family trip to the Philippines last year that cost over $5,000.

— **Rod Dyquiangco**

If I have the money—I buy it—otherwise I save for it and the item is a treat. If it's too expensive (like a new van), I finance it.

— **Daryl Daley**

P.S. A few comments "by the people."

Chapter 5
Deal Or No Deal
GETTING A GOOD DEAL

"This wasn't quite what I expected when they said *small monthly payments*."

Let's make a deal! It's a great deal! What a deal! What's the big deal?! Deal me in. Deal me out. No deal. What is the *deal*? And how do we know if we are getting a *good* deal?

We have a limited amount of money to use. So naturally we want to get the best value for our money. That's what we are exploring in this chapter. And when we ask, "Deal or no deal?" we want you to be able to answer, "DEAL."

Fix it up, wear it out; make it do or do without

The pioneers had a motto: Fix it up, wear it out; make it do, or do without. Not a very popular sentiment in today's consumer culture. Of course, the pioneers didn't have a lot of options. There wasn't a mall on the corner where they could buy the latest fashions and even if there were, money was an issue. So, I guess we have at least one thing in common. The difference is that we don't let *lack* of money stop us from buying it anyway…at least that *was* the case in the past. Now, we know our limits and we stay within them; but inside the limits there is some room to maneuver. That's what finding a good deal is all about.

We are talking about being frugal, not cheap. They're not the same thing. If we sacrifice quality for a lower price we won't be much farther ahead—we will end up having to replace the item at least once, and possibly again and again. If we buy things we don't need and won't use, even if they are inexpensive, we have just wasted our money. (Check your kitchen cupboards and your clothes closets.)

There is something to be said for the pioneers' motto. If you can follow their example and make your own things you can save a lot. There is a time cost of course. We suppose this is as good a time as any to talk about the value of time. You can pay someone to do something that you can't, or don't want to do for yourself. If you can do it yourself and save $30 but could, and would, spend that time working and earn $60, it probably would make more sense to pay someone else to do it for you. (We are entirely discounting the satisfaction of doing it yourself, of course. Sometimes money shouldn't even be a consideration.)

Money Talks

Deal or no deal

According to thefreedictionary.com, the word deal has several meanings. One of those definitions suits our purpose: "A sale, favorable especially to the buyer; a bargain."

http://www.thefreedictionary.com/deal

Today there is a game show called "Deal or No Deal." A contestant initially chooses 1 of 26 suitcases, each with a hidden cash value ranging from $.01 to $1,000,000. As the game continues, the player has to choose suitcases which are opened to reveal the cash value—attempting to avoid the higher value cash amounts. Along the way (after a certain number of suitcases are opened) the "banker" will offer money to induce the player to stop playing the game. The contestant must agree, "deal," or refuse, "no deal." The game ends when the last suitcase is opened or the player takes the *deal*. The contestant doesn't know if he's made a good deal until all amounts are revealed.

Let's look at an example. Everyone has to eat but perhaps cooking is not on your list of favorite things to do. You could grin and bear it and cook anyway. You may decide that your time would be better spent doing other things so you may choose to eat out every night—an expensive choice. Or you could order pre-made meals that will be delivered to your home. Obviously, you have to pay for this service—you don't want to do it for yourself, why would anyone else? Is this new cost justified? Is it worth paying for this service? You may choose instead to buy "heat and serve" or frozen entrees; still more expensive than cooking from scratch but these options save time and effort. You may get even more creative and join a group to exchange meals or do your own big batch cooking and make your own meals to store in the freezer.

When you take into account the time involved, the effort, (the bother) and your own abilities, you can figure out what options are worth your time and money. Anyway, back to our discussion…

If you have invested in good quality items they can be "fixed up or worn out" because they will last and stay in style. For example, clothes that are purchased in a classic style can be altered or worn with other pieces. They will last for years through different clothing trends and styles and normal wear and tear.

Let's make a deal

There are some other techniques to consider. Bartering is a way of exchanging goods or services for other goods and services, without using any money. You may already have a barter system set up. Perhaps you exchange babysitting hours with another couple. You may do sewing for someone who will do some house painting for you. Bartering can extend from exchanging goods or business services to home exchanges, or vehicle swaps. Beware—there may be tax implications. We recommend that you check with your accountant.

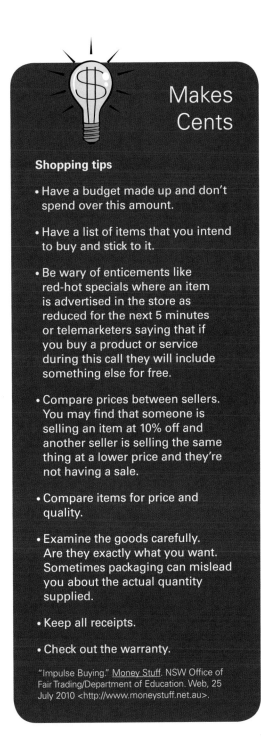

Makes Cents

Shopping tips

• Have a budget made up and don't spend over this amount.

• Have a list of items that you intend to buy and stick to it.

• Be wary of enticements like red-hot specials where an item is advertised in the store as reduced for the next 5 minutes or telemarketers saying that if you buy a product or service during this call they will include something else for free.

• Compare prices between sellers. You may find that someone is selling an item at 10% off and another seller is selling the same thing at a lower price and they're not having a sale.

• Compare items for price and quality.

• Examine the goods carefully. Are they exactly what you want. Sometimes packaging can mislead you about the actual quantity supplied.

• Keep all receipts.

• Check out the warranty.

"Impulse Buying." Money Stuff. NSW Office of Fair Trading/Department of Education. Web, 25 July 2010 <http://www.moneystuff.net.au>.

Your Money's Worth

Wampum

The term "wampum" may be derived from the Wampanoag word, Wampumpeag, which means white shell beads.

When Europeans came to the Americas, they realized the importance of wampum to Native people. While the Native people did not use it as money, the New England colonies used it as a medium of exchange. Soon, they were trading with the native peoples of New England and New York using wampum. The New England colonies demonetized wampum in 1663. Meanwhile it continued as currency in New York at the rate of eight white, or four black, wampum equaling one stuiver (5 cent Dutch coin) until 1673. The colonial government issued a proclamation setting the rate at six white or three black to one penny. This proclamation also applied in New Jersey and Delaware. The black shells were considered worth more than the white shells, which led people to dye the latter, and diluted the value of the shells. The ultimate basis for their value was their redeemability for pelts from the Native Americans. As Native Americans became reluctant to exchange pelts for the shells, the shells lost value.

Their use as common currency was phased out in New York by the early 1700s.

"Wampum." Wikipedia, The Free Encyclopedia. Wikimedia Foundation, Inc. 27 June 2010. Web, 5 July 2010 <http://en.wikipedia.org/wiki/Wampum>.

We often think of haggling as a practice most commonly used outside of North America. "Bargaining or haggling is a type of negotiation in which the buyer and seller of a good or service dispute the price which will be paid and the exact nature of the transaction that will take place, and eventually come to an agreement." ("Bargaining." Wikipedia, The Free Encyclopedia. Wikimedia Foundation, Inc. 3 July 2010. Web, 31 July 2010 <http://en.wikipedia.org/wiki/Haggling>.) Most of us would not think about paying the asking price at a yard sale but are not comfortable with the thought of *negotiating* with store personnel over prices. It can be a profitable use of time, however, especially for expensive items. Check out some pointers in our additional resources section on the website.

Ask for a discount when buying a floor model (the item that's on display and has been handled by shoppers). You can also try just asking for a better price. You never know what you could save until you try.

How about getting something for free? Make your own *wish list* to share with family members and friends who are looking for gift ideas for your birthday or other special occasions. If someone else buys it for you, that's even better. But, if you run out of people who are willing to buy you things, what are your other options? Where else can you get good things for less?

First, obviously, you can check flyers for sale items. Coupons, refunds and rebates are available in-store and online. A little research can save you hundreds of dollars on your purchases. You may have to spend some time on the computer, print off a coupon from the Internet, or mail in a rebate form. A little effort, maybe just a few minutes of your time, can yield a great reward.

Don't forget to take advantage of competitor's coupons or price matching between *like* stores to get a better price on a key item. Bring the competitor's flyer with you when you shop so that you have proof-in-hand when you ask for a discount.

Some stores allow you the price match discount even after the purchase is made (perhaps up to 30 days later). Ask what the store's policy is and the refund procedure. If you see a lower price after the purchase is made then bring in the flyer and your receipt to get the refund.

Did you know that there is a best time to purchase many items? Think about off-season, or end of season, or after the thrill is gone. For example the best time to buy:

Air conditioners: winter (Obviously, who else wants them when it's already cold?)

Big Appliances: September and October clearance when the new models come in

Bicycles and outdoor gear: January, again, not prime outdoor season

Cars: September, before the new models come; also end of month to meet quotas

Clothing: February and September; end of season sales

Computers: July and August or when a new model is launched

Cookware: April, May for weddings; October, November for the holidays

Electronics: 6 months after the hype; in the spring when the store wants to clear out the old to make room for the new stuff

Furniture: January and July have the best clearance deals

Gas grills: winter, not prime barbeque season

Jewelry: not holidays, there's no incentive to lower the prices at these times

Linens and bedding: January, traditional white sales time

Real Estate: winter, when others don't want to look

Recreational vehicles: fall and winter, before the *play* months

Toys: August, end of season; before and after the holidays

TVs: end of summer, beginning of fall or pre- and post-holiday sales

Vacuum cleaners: April and May before the new models are out

Wedding: winter, not the most popular season for weddings; Friday nights and Sundays

Wedding gowns: November and December; end of season

Apparently timing is everything, even when you are making purchases!

Buyer Beware

So-called "affordable" luxuries

The Bagsnob recently alerted us to a bit of fashion insanity: A leading American designer and maker of luxury lifestyle handbags has put a $10,000 price tag on an alligator-skin handbag. Those who commented on the post were justifiably shocked and befuddled, and demanded to know if the execs at said design house had lost their minds.

We, too, wondered if they'd gone off the deep end, but were determined to uncover the method behind their madness—and we found at least one good explanation on WSJ.com (Ok, maybe not good but certainly apt): Luxury brands apparently need to create high-priced anchor items in order to woo consumers into purchasing their lower-end, and hence "affordable luxury" items instead.

In other words, the marketing minds at many luxury fashion brands would like you to covet the high-ticket items, then satisfy your needs by purchasing a lower-priced albeit still expensive bag, wallet or even a keychain instead as a sort of consolation prize. The takeaway? Life's little treats are grand but ask yourself if you aren't just buying something for the label when a less expensive item of similar quality would suffice.

"The Psychology Behind Affordable Luxury." The Budget Babe. Dianna Baros. Web, 28 July 2010 <http://www.thebudgetbabe.com/archives/193-The-Psychology-Behind-Affordable-Luxury.html>.

Don't "discount" dollar stores

Another source for low-cost items is the dollar store.

Penny: I thought you said don't buy cheap?

Author: The dollar store has changed—more, more, more—more organized, more products, and more quality items. There are many items that you might find in large department stores but at much reduced prices. Some of the most popular choices of shoppers include:

- *cleaning products*
- *candy*
- *spices*
- *bath products*
- *gift wrap and gift bags*
- *scrapbooking supplies*
- *containers*
- *household items*
- *kitchen gadgets and utensils*
- *children's books*
- *craft supplies*
- *school supplies*
- *office supplies*
- *glassware*

Penny: I think I'll go shopping.

We do recommend you use caution as some of the products are imported from countries that don't have the same manufacturing and safety standards that we have in our country. Be careful with food items, especially. Check ingredients and expiry dates. Use your good judgment. Saving a little money at the expense of your health isn't a good deal.

Common Cents

"What we need are not only a few simple steps to get us on the right track but also the ability to STAY on that track. Before you think to yourself, 'I need more money,' think about making the most of what you already have."

- Ben Leonard

"A bargain is something you can't use at a price you can't resist."

- Franklin Jones

Also, safety is a concern. Beware of some dangerous look-alike products. Children's toys, toothpaste, make-up, batteries, electrical devices, vitamins, metal jewelry, etc. (you get the idea) may not be items that should be on your dollar store shopping list.

Secondhand rose

For those of you who don't mind buying secondhand (previously enjoyed, once-around-the-block, used good, pre-loved) items, you can get some great deals!! What's more, you are recycling and keeping things from going to the landfill. And when you buy from non-profit thrift stores, you help the disabled and disadvantaged in your own neighborhood. On a wider scale, these organizations provide disaster relief and other good works nationally and globally.

There is a proviso, of course. Some things should not be purchased secondhand—ever. And some other purchases must be approached with extreme caution. There are potentially SERIOUS safety issues involved. Consider this partial list: electrical tools, halogen floor lamps, car jacks, life jackets, helmets and other protective sports devices, swimming pools and fences, baby equipment (like car seats, cribs, carriers, playpens, play yards, accordion-style safety gates), kids' clothes with drawstrings, bunk beds, some toys, mattresses, bean bags with zippers and **any items on a recall list**.

With that in mind, here are some sources for secondhand goods: the classified section of the newspaper, auctions, estate sales, yard sales, church rummage sales, pawn shops, flea markets, thrift stores, vintage stores, secondhand stores, consignment stores, recycling centers and online sites. Obviously, the advantage of buying secondhand is being able to save money buying things you need.

There used to be a stigma around shopping at thrift stores. It seems that things have changed. Today people like to boast about their "finds." I've heard many women respond to a compliment about what she is wearing with "I got it at ___ and it only cost me ___." Besides, it's really *in* to go green and save the planet by reusing our resources. Save money, save the planet and look good!!

Your Money's Worth

"Previously-enjoyed" items that are a good deal

- DVDs and CDs

- books

- video games

- clothing: special occasion clothing, holiday attire, maternity and baby and children's clothes

- jewelry/accessories

- games

- musical instruments: for a beginner musician

- pets

- home decorating pieces

- craft supplies

- furniture

- hand tools

- sports equipment

- gardening supplies

- cars/recreational items

Remember—safety first. Your health and well-being trump price—always.

But it's possible to get even better deals. How about a few tips from experienced buyers:

Auctions: Research, inspect and set your bidding limit—sales are legally binding.

Yard sales: Make a list, bring cash, bargain and research beforehand so you can recognize *finds*. "Better" neighborhoods may have the same stuff but at higher prices.

Flea Markets: Buying on the last day or in the last hours of a sale might give you great deals as sellers want to get rid of their merchandise and are willing to lower their prices. Bundle several items in order to negotiate a better price.

Thrift stores: They may have discount days (for seniors) and big sale days.

Consignment stores: They may reduce prices on an item the longer it is in the store. They also have end of season sales.

Online: Buying online saves time, money and gas.

Retail stores: Floor models are often discounted and video stores will discount previously-viewed movies.

We can't cover everything in this chapter. There are resources to help you get a better deal on your cell phone plans, compare car insurance rates and mortgage loan rates, print off coupons and get promotional codes, find used items, and compare prices of just about anything you could think of to buy, and on and on. And we are pretty confident that at this point you know where to go to find the links…and we encourage you to share your resources with us so that we can pass them on.

Let's look at a couple of specific examples of big ticket items and talk about how you can get better deals.

Home sweet home

Everyone has to live somewhere. Not everyone wants to own their own home—some people are happy to rent; home ownership is a big responsibility. At some point you may think about purchasing a home. When is the right time to purchase a home? Timing is important. (Some would say timing is *everything*.) Answer the questions on the next page before you make your decision.

Buyer Beware

Impulse buying

Impulse buying happens when you get caught up in the hype of a situation and you buy something without thinking much about it. Impulse items may be new products, samples or well-established products at unexpected low prices. Situations that play on shoppers' impulsiveness include: items on sale tables that advertise "huge bargains" or "10% off all items" or the enticement of announcements that something is half price for the next 5 minutes. Impulse buying makes you spend money on items you may not really need or want. To avoid impulse buying you need to ask yourself if you really need the item or just want it.

"Impulse Buying." Money Stuff. NSW Office of Fair Trading/Department of Education. Web, 25 July 2010 <http://www.moneystuff.net.au>.

Are you one of those who should rent and not buy? Here are some things to consider:

- **Credit score.** What is your credit score? If a potential lender sees a bad credit score you may not even qualify for a loan. Or you may have to pay higher rates offered by lenders who are willing to take a higher risk.

- **Debt ratios.** Lenders will look at two debt ratios: front-end and back-end. (See chapter 3.) If the debt ratio is high you may not qualify for a loan. Again if you *could* find a lender, the interest rates would be higher.

- **Job stability.** How stable is your job? Many companies are laying off, downsizing or going broke. How would you continue to make mortgage payments if you lost your job?

- **Relocation.** Will you be staying in the same location for at least 2 or 3 years? If you are planning to move, you probably won't be able to recover the costs of buying and selling, and that's in a rising market. If the market goes down…

- **Home costs.** The cost of a home does not end at the purchase. There are repairs and routine maintenance costs incurred every year. Can you do the work yourself—do you want to do the work yourself? If not, can you afford to hire someone else? You have to leave room in your budget for these expenses.

- **Renting costs.** It may make more sense to rent in the area you want to live in if the cost of owning a home (mortgage payment, property taxes, etc.) is significantly higher than the cost of renting.

- **Extra closing costs.** In addition to the house price, there are real estate agent commissions, lawyer fees, land transfer taxes and a host of other hidden fees that will be added to the total *cost* of buying a house when you make your home purchase.

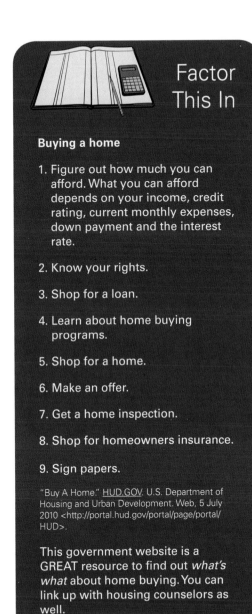

Factor This In

Buying a home

1. Figure out how much you can afford. What you can afford depends on your income, credit rating, current monthly expenses, down payment and the interest rate.

2. Know your rights.

3. Shop for a loan.

4. Learn about home buying programs.

5. Shop for a home.

6. Make an offer.

7. Get a home inspection.

8. Shop for homeowners insurance.

9. Sign papers.

"Buy A Home." HUD.GOV. U.S. Department of Housing and Urban Development. Web, 5 July 2010 <http://portal.hud.gov/portal/page/portal/HUD>.

This government website is a GREAT resource to find out *what's what* about home buying. You can link up with housing counselors as well.

Do The Math

0% financing: a good deal?

While 0% financing offers are enticing, you should read the fine print and know the facts before you head off to your local dealer. Teaser rates such as 0% rates have always been offered to drive more business to the car dealers, but often, 0% offers are not beneficial to everyone. The variations of interest rate, like pricing, can change from dealership to dealership, but knowing what to look for and which questions to ask the dealer will help you decide if a 0% auto loan is the best deal for you. Here are a few of the facts and restrictions that often apply:

• Almost perfect credit may be needed to qualify for 0% car loans.

• You may be required to give up a manufacturer's rebate to get 0% financing.

• 0% financing usually means shorter loan terms and often large monthly payments.

• 0% rates are usually offered on a limited number of models.

• You may be limited to dealer stock and not be able to choose the exact vehicle you are interested in purchasing with 0% auto financing.

"0% Auto Financing." My Auto Loan. Web, 30 June 2010 <http://www2.myautoloan.com/site/page/pg4665-as68-pn_0_Auto_Financing.html>.

If you've answered the questions on the previous page and feel like you should buy a house but are still worried about whether or not you can afford it, try this experiment. Pretend that you have purchased the house you want. If the new mortgage and property taxes would be $1300/month and you are currently paying $700/month in rent, then put the $600 difference into savings. How are you managing? If it isn't a hardship then you can probably handle the costs of home ownership. If it's too tight then think about a lower-priced property and/or continue to save the difference and increase the down payment on your future home. Both of these options will lower your future mortgage payment.

A licensed realtor, a mortgage broker, your banker or financial advisor can help you work out the numbers. Get your mortgage pre-approved. Before purchasing, have the property inspected by a professional—you don't want a lot of unexpected and expensive costs. Remember, you don't have to use the entire amount that a lender is willing to lend you. Being comfortable and having breathing room is an important factor in your financial happiness. After all, the size of the house doesn't make a house a "home." Less financial stress = happier families in our experience.

To lease or not to lease

Leasing a car is similar to renting a house; you make payments each month but don't ever end up owning anything. Why would anyone lease a vehicle, instead of purchasing one? There are some advantages such as a low down payment, lower monthly payments (than if you were financing a purchase) and at the end of the lease you can just return the car and take your brand new vehicle (and new lease) with you.

An attractive feature of new cars is the warranty program, which typically covers the first three years. Many vehicles will be under warranty for the length of the lease. This can give some peace of mind in case the vehicle needs repairs. It is important to follow the manufacturer's recommended maintenance schedule to ensure that your vehicle will be covered under the warranty. You are responsible to cover the maintenance costs and will be on the hook for any repair costs once the warranty expires.

It's not all roses however. When you lease, the vehicle is never paid off. If you decide that you want out of the deal before the lease expires there may be big penalties. Leased vehicles have a maximum mileage/year and when you exceed that amount you have to pay a fee/mile on any excess miles driven. If there is damage to the car beyond what the leasing company considers to be normal wear and tear you will have to pay for the repairs. You may have to purchase extra insurance in case the car is stolen or totaled, as there could be a difference between what the insurance company would pay out and the amount left owing on the lease.

Bill: I've been thinking about leasing a car. I've had my eye on one…and it's a pretty low monthly payment, but I'm still not sure if it's what I should do.

Author: When trying to make the decision about whether you should lease a vehicle, use the checklist in the sidebar.

You may want to lease if you want to free up cash flow; if you want a new car every three years; if you drive 15,000 miles/year or less; if you keep your vehicles in good condition; if you will use the vehicle for business; and if you want to be able to lock in the resale value of the vehicle.

You may not want to lease if you expect changes in your life: job, home or relationships; if you are not comfortable with the lease company; if the lease company doesn't offer gap insurance, and you don't want to pay for that insurance coverage yourself; if the buy-out option is not at a fixed price.

If you don't understand what you are getting into, then don't lease!

Bill: I guess the bottom line is that I need to check it out thoroughly before I make a decision.

Bank On It

Should I lease?

1. If cash flow is an issue, leasing may make more sense for you, as your monthly payments will be lower than if you buy.

2. If you want a new car every three years, leasing gives you the *new car* smell, the latest safety features, and the vehicle warranty.

3. When leasing it is best to stay within 15,000 miles/year. Also, it's important that the car stays in good condition. Do you fit the bill?

4. If you will use the vehicle for business, the tax deduction will be higher with lease payments—though there is a cap for luxury vehicles.

5. When you lease you lock in the residual (resale) value at the end of your lease.

6. Leasing requires some degree of stability in your life. If you foresee changes coming, don't lease.

7. How comfortable are you with the company that you will lease from? Leasing is complex. Choose a company that is interested in having you come back.

8. If the lease company doesn't offer gap insurance, you could get hit with big costs if the vehicle is stolen or totaled. You would have to pay for that insurance coverage yourself.

9. If you think you might purchase—or want the option—at the end of the lease, make sure the buyout option is at a fixed price.

Your Money's Worth

How to shop smart

- **Decide upon your needs.** Learn to live with less.

- **Make your own style.** Why follow the crowd?

- **Have style.** Choose your outfits carefully.

- **Extend your wardrobe.** Coordinate your clothes into a month's worth of outfits.

- **Make a plan.** Determine what you need to complete an outfit.

- **Be sure it's exceptional.** Check for quality, color, fit and a long-lasting style.

- **Compare clearance prices online.** Have a rough idea of what you're willing to pay.

- **Try the flea market.** You'll find a variety of unique imported and secondhand items.

- **Try the dollar store.** Their selection may be limited, but they have cute clothes and accessories.

- **Try thrift stores.** Vintage is always in fashion. Brand names can be found.

- **Watch for sales.** Use coupons...try things on prior to a sale. Take time to think things over....

- **Bring a limited amount of cash.** Stay within your budget. Leave credit cards at home.

- **Do not remove the tags.** Wait a week to think it over.

Adapted from an article provided by WikiHow. "How To Shop Smart." Wikihow. Web, 20 July 2010 <http://www.wikihow.com/Shop-Smart>.

Online purchases

Just one last word before we end this chapter. As we go to the Internet for more and more of our shopping needs, it's important that we keep our personal information safe.

Here are some safety tips:

- **Web browser**. Use the security features of your web browser.

- **Secure websites**. Use websites that are secure. Look for https: in the website address and the padlock or key symbol in the browser window.

- **Online-only credit card number**. Some credit card companies offer numbers that are used for online purchases only. Otherwise, keep one credit card that you only use for this purpose.

- **Paypal**. If you set up an account using your credit or debit card with Paypal, you can use it to pay for your purchases at many online retailers. This way you don't have to give your personal information out to all the stores where you want to make purchases. The Paypal system is free, it's secure and your information is not shared with anyone else.

- **Passwords**. Have a secure password that you use only for your online purchases, and don't use the "save the password" feature.

- **Reputable companies**. Only use companies that you are familiar with.

- **Better Business Bureau online**. Review the database of security features of online registered sites, and customer reviews.

- **Credit only**. No cash, debit or checks—credit only for online purchases. Customers are protected against fraudulent use of their credit card as well.

- **Log out**. When you are done, log out of the website.

- **Credit card statements**. Track your transactions and then check your statements.

- **Report any suspicious activity or errors.**

We make these suggestions:

- Fix it up, wear it out; make it do or do without.

- Learn the fine art of haggling, bargaining and negotiating.

- Check out your local dollar stores.

- Buy secondhand for great savings.

- Figure out if buying or renting a home is best for you.

- Compare leasing to buying a vehicle.

- Safety first when making online purchases.

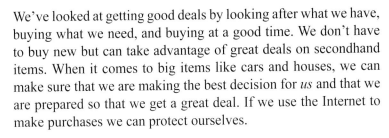

We've looked at getting good deals by looking after what we have, buying what we need, and buying at a good time. We don't have to buy new but can take advantage of great deals on secondhand items. When it comes to big items like cars and houses, we can make sure that we are making the best decision for *us* and that we are prepared so that we get a great deal. If we use the Internet to make purchases we can protect ourselves.

Okay, enough about us…let's talk about our children and how we can meet some of their needs…

Fool's Gold

Protect yourself from counterfeiting and piracy

The U.S. Department of Commerce and U.S. Chamber of Commerce recommend these 10 easy steps you can take to keep your business and home safe from fakes:

- Scrutinize labels, packaging, and contents.

- Seek authorized retailers.

- Watch for missing sales tax charges.

- Insist on secure transactions.

- Seek quality assurance in the secondary market.

- Report questionable spam and faulty products.

- Be vigilant when buying abroad.

- Teach your kids about counterfeits.

- Warn friends and family of illegitimate product sources.

- Trust your instincts.

"Top 10 Ways To Protect Yourself From Counterfeiting And Piracy." Stop Fakes. International Trade Administration. Web, 23 July 2010 <http://www.stopfakes.gov/pdf/Consumer_Tips.pdf>.

Web sites used in the chapter

http://bit.ly/cXC2EW	(TheFreeDictionary.com) A definition of "deal."
http://bit.ly/cjRflC	(MoneyStuff.net) "Impulse Buying."
http://bit.ly/crngRx	(Wikipedia) A definition of "bargaining."
http://bit.ly/cNldBp	(Wikipedia) A definition of "wampum."
http://bit.ly/9ZQEGZ	(TheBudgetBabe.com) "The Psychology Behind Affordable Luxury."
http://bit.ly/bgiPPp	(Housing and Urban Development) "Buy A Home."
http://bit.ly/apZgTb	(MyAutoLoan.com) Article about 0% auto financing.
http://bit.ly/bHOi1Q	(WikiHow.com) "How To Shop Smart."
http://bit.ly/drT607	(StopFakes.gov) "Top 10 Ways To Protect Yourself From Counterfeiting And Piracy."

Additional resources

Fix it up, wear it out; make it do or do without

http://bit.ly/bsWBoq	(Woman's Day) A year-long savings program.
http://bit.ly/9LfTHr	(MoneyInstructor.com) Simple money saving tips.
http://bit.ly/deW6jS	(theFind.com) Find coupons from thousands of stores.

Let's make a deal

http://bit.ly/cpjn6j	(u-exchange.com) "Bartering, Exchanging, Trading, Swapping."
http://bit.ly/aw3kgZ	(Readers Digest) "Haggle Like A Pro: 5 Lines That Work."
http://bit.ly/d16dV6	(MSN Money) "The Best Time To Buy...Anything."

Don't 'discount' dollar stores

http://bit.ly/bnHfRh	(About.com) "Top Ten Dollar Store Deals."
http://bit.ly/cBrvmr	(AssociatedContent.com) Are dollar stores really worth it?
http://bit.ly/dcn5vH	(Helium.com) Benefits of shopping at the dollar store.

Secondhand rose

http://bit.ly/cEeadI	(US Consumer Product Safety Commission) Safety standards, recalls, unsafe products.
http://bit.ly/9ekgsN	(theThriftShopper.com) Search for thrift stores.
http://bit.ly/brdVkx	(MoneyInstructor.com) Getting good deals at yard/garage sales.

Home sweet home

http://nyti.ms/c2AFJ4	(New York Times) Rent vs. buy calculator.
http://bit.ly/9TaMll	(USA) (hsh.com) Mortgage caculators and rate compare.
http://bit.ly/bxv4Pn	(Canada) (RateSupermarket.ca) Compare mortgage rates.

To lease or not to lease

http://bit.ly/cq0Two	(LeaseGuide.com) Lease or buy? Which is better?
http://bit.ly/bQP31A	(TrueCar.com) Find out what others paid for their new car.
http://bit.ly/bzRNHb	(MSN Auto) "Ten Tips For Used Car Buying Success."

Online purchases

http://bit.ly/bYwfcM	(PromotionalCodes.com) Promo codes for retailers.
http://bit.ly/bbn3ga	(eBates.com) Discount codes from over 1300 stores.
http://bit.ly/aGaX0z	(PriceProtectr.com) Get notified if price drops during price protection period.

We asked, "How do you get good value for your money?" and you said...

Recently I replaced my kitchen. I bought oak cabinets and high-end Jenn-air appliances. All were gently used. I installed it all with help from family and friends. I bought new countertops and flooring on sale in the summer. To buy the appliances new would have been $7,000 including tax. I paid $2,000. The cabinets would be $8,000-$10,000, I paid $1500. By the time I was finished I spent approx. $7,000 and I now have a $20,000+ kitchen.

— **Nancy Gibson**

Never buy new. For cars we look at "Cap Cars" (cars driven for 6 months by auto company execs) and save 40 to 50%. On houses being sold because auto execs got transferred, we save 20 to 30%.

— **Kevin Brady**

I have saved literally THOUSANDS of dollars by going to garage sales and almost exclusively buying at thrift stores. I accept ALL hand-me-down clothing for my kids and can honestly count on one hand the number of times I have had to purchase clothes for my kids. My favorite garage sale purchases have included 2 *Group of Seven* paintings (very valuable), a large inflatable backyard pool, a bike trailer, and a canoe. I love to barter and get a real "high" when I have made a killer deal!

— **Lori LaFrance**

What works for me, I don't pay full price for anything. If I want something I will wait for it to go on sale; if it doesn't go on sale I was not meant to have it. But, if I go to the store and it's on sale and in my size, then it was fate.

— **Nichole Caskanette**

Using money for a down payment on a home is the single most important thing you can do regarding money as well as keeping your credit score as good as possible. Good credit means leverage at the bank. Buying and later flipping your home can be the most lucrative source of money you can ever get.

— **Jeremy Dawson**

Prior to the birth of our first child, we went shopping....When we got to the cashier, almost everything was discounted off the ticketed price we saw. Playpen had a slightly damaged box—discounted. Crib was the floor model—discounted. High chair—discounted as sale item and so on. The clerk helped us in the aisle for a while and then discounted most of the items without being asked to....We saved over $200.

— **Dale Albers**

When I'm looking for used items I go to the Internet first. I've found great deals on Kijiji. I've also been able to list items that I wanted to sell on their website and I've found buyers for my unwanted items.

— **B. J.**

By renovating our modest homes, we were able to double our profit [when we sold them].

— **K. Armstrong**

[I've saved money] by having in mind what the price range should be and then comparing prices between different brands. Haggling helps to get the best price.

— **Barbara Anderson**

Your dumbest purchase:

- an exercise machine (which we very seldom use)
- joining a CD club
- gym membership—never used
- buying "knock off" products
- bought new electronics—before the price dropped
- a jean jacket that cost 4 ½ months' salary

Your smartest purchase:

- education
- my house
- everything that is paid for
- engagement and wedding ring for my wife
- good used equipment
- classic style, good quality clothes
- our cottage

For more ideas from people just like you, visit **http://powerspendingbook.com/by-the-people**

Chapter 6

Train Up A Child

TEACHING CHILDREN ABOUT MONEY

"I just asked for five dollars."

Common Cents

"Example is the school of mankind and they will learn at no other."

- **Kurt Herbert Alder**

Money Talks

Train up a child

"Train up a child in the way he should go: and when he is old, he will not depart from it."

Origin

The part we can agree on is that this phrase originated from the Bible, Proverbs 22:6. It was written by King Solomon (Solomon the Wise) three thousand years ago.

What we can't agree on is what the phrase meant originally and what it means today. There is a LOT of heated discussion on the subject.

This is how we choose to interpret it for the purposes of this book: "To train, or to train up, to educate; to teach; to form by instruction or practice; to bring up."

[1913 Webster Dictionary]

Home is the first school our children attend. Our children watch us and form many of their future behaviors based on what they experience during childhood. As parents we have a responsibility to teach our children about the value of money and how to use it properly. We can make their road smoother—not because we are giving them handouts but because we are giving them tools. (We have lots of personal experience on this topic as we have nine children between us!!)

Lead the children

In today's technology-driven society, children may get the impression that "money does grow on trees"—or at least in bank machines which spit out money whenever we insert our card. Or, we hand over a plastic card to a cashier and we take away our *stuff* and not a bill or coin was to be seen anywhere during the entire transaction. There aren't any pay packets at the end of the work week either. Most of us don't even get a check anymore—the money is put directly into our bank account. It may be difficult for children to see the whole financial process in action—though we earn money and we use money to buy things—houses, cars, insurance, investments…most of these transactions are done automatically and invisibly.

Despite appearances, money doesn't grow on trees—at least not in our neighborhood, and children need to be taught about earning an income and spending it. Okay, maybe they understand about spending it…how about spending it wisely…and even saving some?

When children don't have an understanding of how much it costs to run a household, they can be confused and disappointed when they are told that they can't have all the things they want. *Mom and dad can get everything they want, whenever they want, can't they?* You don't want to overcomplicate the whole thing because a younger child won't understand, but it is important to let children be involved in some of the money spending decisions. They are more likely to understand your response to their requests for *stuff*, and may even stop asking, once they do understand.

Teach the children

We decided that we would gather our children together to talk about our family budget. Out came the monopoly money and we counted out the amount we earned in a month. Then we talked about taxes, our expenses and our savings and as we discussed the amount that was spent in each category, we put that amount aside. We kept the categories simple; things that the children could relate to easily. The children could see that a lot of money had to be spent on running the house, and paying for food, clothing, school expenses, and on and on. What we had left was the money to meet our wants. This was a very effective and visual way to explain money management to our children. It opened up the discussion of what we as a family wanted to spend our money on, how we could lower the money spent on variable costs, what we could do that cost less or was free and what things were most important to us.

A family could use this method when introducing a family budget but also when planning vacations, and making entertainment and holiday plans.

When children have money handed to them (or even when they earn it) and are allowed to use it however they want, they don't understand that not all money is disposable income. For adults, disposable income is limited to the after-tax, after-expenses, after-savings amount. Actually, it usually turns out that very little of our money is disposable income.

I tried to explain this concept to my son who had his first full-time job and was still living at home. He paid rent (that's our rule—not in school—living at home—pay rent), and was putting some money aside for savings each paycheck. I noticed that whatever money was *leftover* seemed to get spent.

I urged him to set a budget for his discretionary spending and to save the rest. I told him that he would never have another opportunity like this to put money away. He felt that because he was paying rent, paying his cell phone bill and putting some money into savings, that he had a good handle on money management. Unfortunately he ignored my advice.

Bank On It

Kids and money: the sooner, the better

So when is the best time to start teaching your kids about money? The sooner, the better. In fact, more than 70% of parents believe educating kids about finances should start no later than 1st grade, according to a survey conducted by Northwestern Mutual, a Milwaukee-based insurance company. That's when most kids are 6 or 7 years old.

Many experts say that if your child is old enough to ask for candy or toys, they're old enough to start gaining some financial awareness. Even as soon as they learn to count you can start teaching them about the concept of money using pennies and dollar bills.

But don't despair if your kids are in their teens and you haven't had the "money" talk yet. For you, NOW is the best time to teach your child about money.

That's because teaching children about money is beneficial no matter what their age. As Joline Godfrey, a social worker who founded Independent Means, an organization that teaches children how to manage money, says, "It's developmental, not chronological. You can treat your 15-year-old as a 5- to 8-year-old, teaching them the basic knowledge of financial literacy. It's like learning a new language."

Excerpt from an article from the free SixWise.com Security & Wellness e-Newsletter.
"Kids And Money: 5 Keys To Teaching Kids Money Management Skills." SixWise. Web, 6 July 2010 <http://www.sixwise.com/newsletters/05/02/15/kids_and_money_5_keys_to_teaching_kids_money_management_skills.htm>.

It came as quite a shock when he was on his own, (paying rent, paying for groceries, the Internet, cable, phone, transportation, etc.) that mom was right after all and he wasn't quite as prepared as he thought. "Theory versus reality," as I like to say.

The best way to teach is by example. Children will pay attention to what we do and may not *hear* what we say. Now that you are on the right track financially, you will be able to teach your children how to use money well.

Guide the children

Why not take your children on the same journey that you have just made (modified for the age and understanding level of each child). Talk to them about *wants* versus *needs* and the value of work. Help them set up a simple budget and incorporate savings and charitable giving into the plan. Explain the dangers of credit and debt and help them to learn to make better decisions about their spending (you know, get good value for their money).

We want to elaborate on a few of these points.

Needs versus wants

A discussion of needs and wants should include a talk about *instant* versus *delayed* gratification, peer pressure, and the sense of entitlement that many people feel today.

Perhaps you've heard of the Marshmallow Experiment? It was a study conducted by Walter Mischel in the 1960s and '70s at Stanford University. A group of 4 year olds were given a marshmallow and a bell and told that the researcher was going to leave for a while but if they would wait until the researcher returned before eating the marshmallow they would be given a second marshmallow. If they just couldn't wait, they could ring the bell and the researcher would come back right away. Then they could eat the marshmallow, but they would not get a second one. Some children waited and some did not. Some waited only 30 seconds.

The children's progress was followed into their teenage years. "Once Mischel began analyzing the results, he noticed that low delayers, the children who rang the bell quickly, seemed more likely to have behavioral problems, both in school and at home. They got lower S.A.T. scores. They struggled in stressful situations, often had trouble paying attention, and found it difficult to maintain friendships. The child who could wait fifteen minutes had an S.A.T. score that was, on average, two hundred and ten points higher than that of the kid who could wait only thirty seconds." (Lehrer, Jonah. "Don't!" The New Yorker. 18 May 2009. Web, 6 July 2010 <http://www.newyorker.com/reporting/2009/05/18/090518fa_fact_lehrer>.)

While the results of this study would probably not impress your children, they can understand that *two* "marshmallows" are better than *one*, even if they have to wait a little while to get them. It doesn't hurt a child to have to wait. It builds character, teaches patience and self-control.

"Peer pressure refers to the influence exerted by a peer group in encouraging a person to change his or her attitudes, values, or behavior in order to conform to group norms…Peer pressure can cause people to do things they would not normally do, e.g. take drugs, smoke, get a girlfriend, marry, [get] a job, [have] children, buy expensive items they don't really need (cars, houses, boats, etc.)." ("Peer Pressure." Wikipedia, The Free Encyclopedia. Wikimedia Foundation, Inc. 2 July 2010. Web, 6 July 2010 <http://en.wikipedia.org/wiki/Peer_pressure>.)

Our children may feel that they have to wear a certain label, or own a particular device, and may make our lives miserable until they do. Give your kid tools to fight against negative peer pressure. If your children are confident about who they are and have a strong feeling of their own self-worth, they won't have to rely on their friends' approval to feel good about themselves and they will be less likely to succumb to this pressure.

We want to make one last point under this heading. We have moved from being members of a society that spurned *hand outs* and *charity* for even basic needs, to members of a society that feel *entitled* to luxuries. Our children are being swept up in the "I-must-have-everything-and-I-must-have-it-now" attitude of our society, with the additional feeling of "I-deserve-it." This doesn't make for happier, more productive, more deserving people—it creates a generation of spoiled, lazy and ungrateful people.

Bank On It

Secrets to help your kids handle peer pressure

- Listen compassionately, not judgmentally.

- Don't back down from your values.

- Teach children to stand up for themselves.

- Encourage your child's self-esteem.

- Praise your child for doing the right thing.

Excerpt reprinted with the permission of: Bottom Line Productions Boardroom Inc. Samalin, Nancy. "Secrets To Help Your Kids Handle Peer Pressure." Bottom Line Secrets. 1 August 1977. Web, 6 July 2010 <http://www.bottomlinesecrets.com/article.html?article_id=7297>.

Children grow into adults—what kind of adults do you want them to become? Kids leaving home and expecting to maintain their parents' standard of living (parents who have been accumulating assets for decades) will be sorely disappointed. Remember, if they develop a sense of entitlement, they'll be coming to *you* when they can't afford all the things they want!!

What is our responsibility to our adult children?—*legally*, nothing. Only dependent children (usually under 18) have a claim on their parents. Are you planning to leave an inheritance for your children? Or are you planning to spend it all, if you have time? In any case, do you want your adult children to be dependent on you? Certainly even if you want to leave your adult children something, you shouldn't give up your own comfort to provide it. If there's something left, fine, but we believe we shouldn't have our kids count on a windfall or a bail-out from us. Children should prepare for their own lives and pay for them without counting on their parents to get them through.

Perhaps we need to help children refocus. Let's be realistic. We are some of the most fortunate people on the face of the earth. "At least 80% of the world's population lives on less than $10 a day." (Shah, Anup. "Poverty Facts And Stats." Global Issues. 28 March 2010. Web, 21 July 2010 <http://www.globalissues.org/article/26/poverty-facts-and-stats>.) Help your children to realize how blessed they are and to think about others who are less fortunate. We can guarantee that you won't run out of examples.

When people spend less time thinking about themselves and more about others, they are happier—statistics prove it. Encourage your children to help others by contributing money, or sharing time and talents. A little goes a long way. We'll share some ideas about how you can give to others in chapter 12. Include your children as you give service and everyone will be happier!

Value of work

Children are part of a family. Every household must be maintained and as part of a family, everyone should participate and contribute to its maintenance, based on age and ability of course. Since each family member is a part of the household and has a share in the responsibilities, each should also have a share in the household income.

The level of participation in the household chores and how that participation is recognized is different from household to household, of course. This brings up the topic of allowances.

Penny: Bill and I were wondering if we should pay our kids an allowance. They are still very young.

Author: Many children get an allowance. Some allowances are connected to chores, some aren't. While most children, hopefully ALL children, have chores, (even young children can contribute) completing those chores may not be related to getting an allowance.

Some parents give a fixed allowance but only when chores are completed, some give a fixed allowance and top it up as chores are done, and others have no fixed allowance and just pay their children for certain chores and other job assignments. You must work out the best system for your family.

In any case, there is no doubt that chores teach children both how to work and the rewards of work. The added bonus is that children will learn transferable skills and good work habits that they will be able to use throughout their lives.

Penny: Okay, thanks. And I bet if I want some ideas about age-appropriate chores and allowances I can always go to the additional resources section?

Author: By George, I think you've got it! And don't forget to check out the sidebar for more insight on the subject of children and allowances.

Factor This In

Should children earn their allowance?

By giving kids an allowance for doing chores or helping out around the house, some experts feel like they are missing out on the valuable experiences that come with doing chores simply because you are a part of the family, including cooperation and a sense of duty to help chip in.

In addition, if allowances are tied to expenses such as school lunches or supplies, it can be difficult to enforce the consequences—you don't want the kids to go without lunch because they didn't clean their rooms.

As kids get older, they often get money from other sources, such as babysitting or part-time after school jobs. When this happens, the money they are getting from other sources is often more than the allowance, so kids may start to neglect their chores. Not tying chores to an allowance gives kids a sense of duty in order to help out around the house with the family. If kids are only in it for the money, they are missing out on that important lesson.

Most experts will agree that having children earn their allowance is not a good idea, as it takes away from the feeling of responsibility to help out around the house. As an alternative, you could give kids a chance to earn extra money by doing extra work or chores around the house.

"Should Children Earn Their Allowance?" Surf Net Parents. Barbara J. Feldman. Web. 6 July 2010 <http://www.surfnetparents.com/should_children_earn_their_allowance-2287.html>.

Makes Cents

What jobs can kids do to earn money?

- babysitting/parent helper

- lawn care/landscaping

- snow shoveling

- pet care/dog walking

- car washing

- house cleaning

- have a paper route

- work in the family business

- tutor

- farm work

- summer camp counselor

- pet/house sitting

These suggestions are just *suggestions*. You know your child's age, experience, abilities and interests. You should guide your children when they are looking for ideas for work; your childrens' well being and safety are the most important considerations. Encourage their desire to work but be there to offer guidance.

Eric and Robin use a combination of a fixed allowance and a points system with their young children. The children each get a very small weekly amount of fixed allowance that goes directly into a savings account. From that amount they contribute 10% to charity, 40% to savings and they can spend the remaining 50% on whatever they choose. They also earn points for chores they complete and for other good behavior. These points are tracked on a whiteboard that everyone can see. Every few weeks they open the "Poulin Store" where each child is allowed to "cash in" some or all of her points for treats, special outings or money. They are encouraged to set goals and save for some of the bigger items. If a child wants to do something specific, the Poulins will add that item to the "Poulin Store" at some fixed points amount, and the child then has a goal to work towards. It's amazing how helpful children can be when they have a goal they want to reach!

In the article, "Teaching a Work Ethic," the author Marie Hartwell-Walker makes these suggestions for getting family members to pitch in: "First take a look at your own attitudes about household tasks. Make sure that everyone, adults and kids alike, does a fair share. Whenever possible, do chores together. Make chores routine and regular. Make consequences a lesson in reciprocity. When everyone helps, there's time to do things that people want to do." (Hartwell-Walker, Marie. "Teaching A Work Ethic." Psychcentral. Web, 6 July 2010 <http://psychcentral.com/lib/2006/teaching-a-work-ethic/2>.)

At some point children are ready to move beyond the four walls of the house and get a *real* job (so it's not just *recycled* household money but **new** money). Paper routes, babysitting jobs, part-time jobs, working for neighbors, or running a small business (for the more entrepreneurial youth) are good choices. It's important that the job doesn't interfere with their schooling. Help them to keep their priorities straight.

A job outside of the home gives children good work experience, can help them to choose a career path, teaches money skills, builds confidence, and again, can develop transferable skills for future employment.

Budget

Teach your kids how to budget. If they learn to stick to a budget on their small income, they will be better prepared to handle a larger income down the road. Don't make the mistake of allowing them to spend everything they earn. Sit down with them and go over what they earn and what expenses they are expected to pay out of that amount. Perhaps they will be responsible for buying their own toys or covering their entertainment costs.

As they get older they may be expected to pay for their own clothing or personal care items. Generally, the more money that a child earns, the more personal expenses they should be expected to pay for out of their income.

This is the time when some hard lessons can be learned. If they spend all of their income, or run short, then they will have to do without. It may mean that they can't join their friends for a movie at the theater because they overspent on a pair of jeans. This is a natural consequence of not following the budget. It hurts but that's the point, isn't it? Allow your children to practice for real life in a safe environment.

Savings

We all have to save up for things that we want—larger items, education costs, a down payment on a house, a vehicle and retirement. We might as well get our kids in the saving habit now. You could require a fixed amount or a percentage that must be put aside from every pay that your child receives. It is a forced savings program—they'll thank you for it later, trust us! Some parents or relatives offer to match any savings that a child is putting aside when children are saving to make a larger purchase in the future. This system can make a seemingly impossible goal more attainable.

When we have to save up for something and we pay for it ourselves, we put more value on the item than if it was just given to us. We realize just how much hard work had to be done to earn it. As a result, we usually will take better care of it.

Your Money's Worth

How to buy children's clothing on a budget

Parents know that children are expensive! Buying clothing can be especially draining because they grow out of them so quickly....Any parent can learn to spend much less money on clothes for their children....

Get organized! Take an inventory of what your children already have.

Sell old clothes. Bring your children's gently used clothes to a consignment or re-sale shop....You may be able to get store credit or even cash....You can also sell your children's clothing online.

Take advantage of hand-me-downs.

Shop secondhand. Especially when your child is too young to care...buy secondhand!

Consider wearability. Never, ever buy something that your child will not wear.

Avoid impulse buys! Come armed with information about what you need and where the sales are, and you will be much less likely to fall for the impulse buying trap.

Give old clothes a new life. There are many ways to make children's clothing look new, fashionable, or less boring.

Done well, shopping for clothes can be a great way to show your child the value of money as well as spending some quality time together.

Harris, Bronwyn. "How To Buy Children's Clothing On A Budget." How To Do Things. Web, 6 July 2010 <http://www.howtodothings.com/fashion-personal-care/how-to-buy-childrens-clothing-on-a-budget>.

Buyer Beware

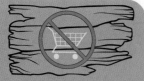

Kids and credit cards

There are some basic ground rules you should insist your [teenager] follow:

1. Never apply for a card without your knowledge.

2. Never have more than one card.

3. Use the card carefully limiting it's use to emergencies or purchases that you both agree on in advance.

4. Use the card as you would a checking account. Keep tabs on any usage by either tracking your balance online, which parents can do as well, or by simply writing it down.

5. Keep the balance as low as possible and pay it off as soon as possible. If you cannot pay the balance off, pay at least twice the minimum payment.

6. Avoid department store cards.

Ironically, these are good rules for parents as well. Teach your children well and you might pick up a few good habits in the process.

Petillo, Paul. "Kids And Credit Cards." Blue Collar Dollar. 7 July 2010 <http://bluecollardollar.com/kids_credit_amnw_081006.html>.

You might introduce credit cards to your student by providing a *prepaid credit card*. Your child will have an opportunity to learn some spending skills but with a built-in safety feature. When the prepaid amount has been spent, the shopping is over!

Getting good value

When you talk to your children about budgeting and putting money aside for savings, this will lead into a discussion about getting good value for your money. You can talk about name brands and the power of advertising. Let your children see that they could spend $50 at one store and get one item or they could wait for a sale and get the same thing for less or buy a different brand and have some money left over. You can also introduce shopping at secondhand stores or at a discount store (refer to our lists in Chapter 5 of course). Maybe they can get 5 or 10 items with their $50.

The daughter of a friend was embarrassed at the thought of shopping at a secondhand store. One day she reluctantly accompanied her mother on a shopping trip to a local consignment store. She browsed around while she waited for her mother and found a gently used pair of boots by a favourite designer for $10. She was sold!! When you know what to look for you can find terrific deals and no one has to know that it's secondhand (though your kids may be tempted to brag about the great deal they got).

Credit and debt

One of our children had his first credit card. We found out that he had just been making minimum payments while continuing to make purchases on the card. When I looked at his credit card statement, I noticed that the interest charge was about the cost of one of the CDs that he loves to collect. When I pointed this out, it made him stop and realize that instead of paying the credit card company interest, he could be adding a CD to his collection each month. It suddenly wasn't just a meaningless number on a piece of paper.

Make this concept of credit and debt understandable—something that your child can relate to. Let him know how long it will take to pay off a credit card debt making just the minimum payment and how much interest will be paid during that time. Now show him what he could have accumulated if he'd saved the interest, instead of paying it!!! Make sure your children understand that when we *owe* something on an item, we don't really *own* it.

Educate the children

Educating your children about money and finances is important and it leads nicely into the next, and last, topic in this chapter: the importance of education in general.

A person's level of education has a direct correlation with future earnings: "A person with a Bachelor's degree will earn, on average, almost twice as much as workers with a high school diploma, over a lifetime ($2.1 million compared to $1.2 million). This is a result of not only higher starting salaries for people with higher education levels, but also the sharper earnings growth over the course [of] their careers." ("Value of Education." Earn My Degree. Web, 7 July 2010 <http://www.earnmydegree.com/online-education/learning-center/education-value. html>.)

Of course people would rather earn *more* than *less* money over their lifetime. But getting an education can be costly so it is important to explore career options before deciding on a college course. You don't want your child to get part way through a college course and then decide it was the wrong choice.

Many high schools incorporate a career course in their mandatory curriculum. Students do research and explore different career options that they think they might be interested in pursuing. This can be a helpful tool for making a career choice. High school guidance counsellors are a(n under-used) resource as well. Counselors can guide students towards careers that they are best suited for and can help them to find a college that offers the programs they are looking for, and make sure that they have the necessary prerequisites. Many colleges hold open houses or come into the high schools to meet with students to answer questions about the courses they offer.

There are co-operative education programs that will give your child a taste of what a particular vocation involves. Better to give it a try over a semester and find out then that it's not the right match, or better yet, find out it is a good match. There are apprenticeship programs that can start during high school also—less *in school* time and more *hands-on* time.

A part-time or summer job, may spark an interest in a particular field and may lead into a post-secondary course of study. Take your child on a tour of a college campus and speak with educators. Talk with people who work in the industry. Research online or read books and career guides. Check out the links on our website. If you really get stumped there are companies (it's a paid service) that will evaluate a person's skills and interests and help to narrow the choices to a few particular vocations.

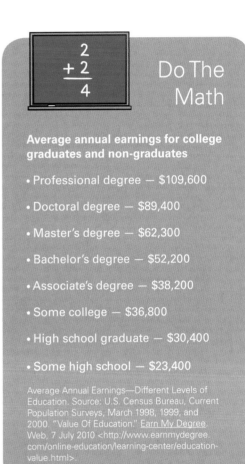

Do The Math

Average annual earnings for college graduates and non-graduates

- Professional degree — $109,600
- Doctoral degree — $89,400
- Master's degree — $62,300
- Bachelor's degree — $52,200
- Associate's degree — $38,200
- Some college — $36,800
- High school graduate — $30,400
- Some high school — $23,400

Average Annual Earnings—Different Levels of Education. Source: U.S. Census Bureau, Current Population Surveys, March 1998, 1999, and 2000. "Value Of Education." Earn My Degree. Web, 7 July 2010 <http://www.earnmydegree. com/online-education/learning-center/education-value.html>.

Once your child picks a course, it has to be paid for. Though the cost of education can be high there is help available.

Bill: *Our kids are young but we're already thinking about their future. Penny and I realize that education is really important but it can also be very expensive. How can we prepare financially to help our kids with their schooling costs?*

Author: Start now and take advantage of government and private education savings plans. There are federal College savings plans—a 529 plan in the U.S. and RESPs in Canada. These plans offer tax benefits and government grants when you make contributions to the plan. Also there are tuition savings plans in each state, and Canada has private scholarship plans. Check for each plan's savings incentives. Grandparents may prefer to put money into an education savings plan for a grandchild rather than buying another toy (that will be added to the pile of other unnecessary and unused toys).

Bill: *I guess we should talk to our advisor and get something started.*

Author: Great idea. It's never too soon.

Factor This In

Education pays...

Level of education	Median weekly earnings In 2009
Doctoral degree	$1532
Professional degree	$1529
Master's degree	$1257
Bachelor's degree	$1025
Associate degree	$761
Some college, no degree	$699
High school graduate	$626
Less than high school	$454

Source: "Education Pays." Bureau of Labor Statistics. 27 May 2010. United States Department of Labor. Web. 7 July 2010 <http://www.bls.gov/emp/ep_chart_001.htm>.

Students may qualify for a scholarship. There are student loan programs, and work programs at colleges for students who have financial needs. There are grants, bursaries, endowments, etc. available. Every college has a financial aid center that can help students through the process of applying for financial aid. Also (as we've said repeatedly) educate yourself, do the research, and take advantage of resources available. There is no reason for any student who is willing and wanting to work hard, not to get an education.

When a student files a tax return there may be credits and/or deductions for education expenses that will help to alleviate some of the costs of getting an education. Anyway, when you weigh present costs against the future rewards you realize that the reward far outweighs the cost. Education can pay back, over and over again!

We make these suggestions:

- Lead your children—set a good *financial* example.

- Teach your children—give them the financial basics.

- Guide your children—take them through the ABCs of money management.

- Educate your children—help them to understand the importance of education.

It is our responsibility to teach our children about finances. The most important thing we can do is to set a good example but we also need to "train them up" by teaching them money basics. We can help our children understand the value of work, how to budget, how to avoid financial traps, how to give and how to save, and how to use their money wisely. We can guide them on their educational path so that they will be able to look after themselves financially in the future. We can show them how to use the resources available to find careers that will be rewarding and profitable.

And if that's not enough to think about, we have more "food for thought" to offer you in our next chapter...

Fool's Gold

Top 8 money mistakes parents make

While new parents are focused on [their baby] long-term financial security is often overlooked. Here are eight of the biggest financial mistakes new parents make.

1. **Overspending on baby.** New parents tend to go overboard in setting up a nursery and buying for baby.

2. **Skimping on life insurance.** Now that you're responsible for another life...take a closer look at your life insurance coverage.

3. **Ignoring disability insurance.** Disability coverage is even more vital because you're statistically more likely to be injured than die while in the workforce.

4. **[Buying] life insurance for your baby.** Don't bother. The only members of your family who need life insurance coverage are those whose death would create a financial hardship.

5. **Delay saving for college.** The best time to start that college fund is when each of your children is born.

6. **Not taking advantage of tax benefits.**

7. **Not making a will.** Parents need a will to designate guardians and an executor.

8. **Forgetting retirement savings.** Too many parents worry about getting their child through college and forget about their own retirement.

Adapted from: "Top 8 Money Mistakes Parents Make." Go Frugal Blog. 23 November 2009. Web, 7 July 2010 <http://www.freeshipping.org/blog/top-8-money-mistakes-parents-make/>.

Web sites used in the chapter

http://bit.ly/9Lfsij	(SixWise.com) "Kids And Money: 5 Keys To Teaching Kids Money Management Skills."
http://bit.ly/cQaDcO	(Zen Habits) "10 Lessons To Teach Your Kids About Money."
http://bit.ly/91otHI	(The New Yorker) The secret of self-control.
http://bit.ly/9rKvQ9	(Wikipedia) A definition of "peer pressure."
http://bit.ly/cuO2fe	(Bottom Line Secrets) "Secrets To Help Your Kids Handle Peer Pressure."
http://bit.ly/boZjah	(GlobalIssues.org) "Poverty Facts And Stats."
http://bit.ly/anJayq	(SurfNetParents.com) "Should Children Earn Their Allowance?"
http://bit.ly/ci3Goz	(PsychCentral.com) "Teaching A Work Ethic."
http://bit.ly/aRi9By	(HowToDoThings.com) "How To Buy Children's Clothing On A Budget."
http://bit.ly/bj64SI	(BlueCollarDollar.com) "Kids And Credit Cards."
http://bit.ly/c9mvWk	(EarnMyDegree.com) Job salary earnings comparison depending on education level.
http://bit.ly/bUV4fn	(US Dept of Labor) Education pays in higher earnings and lower unemployment rates.
http://bit.ly/4Ta9xn	(Go Frugal Blog) "Top 8 Money Mistakes Parents Make."

Additional resources

Lead the children

http://bit.ly/b7xJ64	(ArticleIntelligence.com) "Show Children Strong Money Management Skills."
http://bit.ly/crraW8	(SubmitYourArticle.com) "Show Children The Way."
http://bit.ly/d9z4kI	(ArticleCompilation.com) "All Parents Ought To Show Children The Right Way To Stay In Control Of Their Very Own Finances."

Teach the children

http://bit.ly/bkb8Zt	(FamilyEducation.com) Lessons and resources to teach your children about money.
http://bit.ly/9cYsSE	(PsychologyToday.com) "Therapy Watch: Tight Budget, Tight Lips: Talking To Kids About Family Finances."
http://bit.ly/a4tuEn	(MoneySmarts4Kids.com) Talking To Kids About Family Finances.

Guide the children

http://bit.ly/bTHxdn	(MoneyInstructor.com) Ways for kids to earn money.
http://bit.ly/ddx7T0	(FamilyEducation.com) Info and resources about allowances and chores.
http://bit.ly/c23HLk	(cuno.org) "What Experts Say About Allowances For Children."

Educate the children

http://bit.ly/cU3pVq	(RileyGuide.com) "Explore Career Options."
http://bit.ly/92pahd	(SavingForCollege.com) (USA) Your guide to saving for college.
http://bit.ly/auCTSZ	(eCampus.com) Rent or buy discount books and textbooks.

We asked, "What was the best money lesson you've taught to your family/other?" and you said…

We have young children and when they are given money for holidays and birthdays, we allow them to spend this money—with our supervision. We ask them to decide on what they want and then ask them to give us two reasons for wanting it. We then discuss price and how much they will have left or if they even have enough to buy it in the first place. We also try to wait for a sale. More often than not, by the time this process is concluded, if it was not something that they really, truly wanted, the purchase is not made and they put their money in the bank for a later time.

— **Christena Campanaro**

Teach them to buy once and buy well. I would rather spend more on something and buy the thing I want vs. saving a few dollars and having to repurchase it later.

— **Peter Wowk**

They would always ask for allowance and I would give them jobs to do. If the jobs didn't get done, they didn't get the money. When we went Christmas shopping, I'd give them each a bit of money so they could make small purchases on their own. If they spent it all on one gift they didn't get any more...was there ever a lot of whining with that!! If they wanted money for a school trip, the job list came out again and money would be put aside for the trip as jobs were completed. I have tried again and again to get them to put money away in the bank to save for something they really want and know that nobody is going to get for them. So far, that has gone over like a lead balloon! I guess they just haven't found something they really want. The exception is my oldest daughter. She wanted to go on a school trip to Europe. She knew I couldn't help her pay for it, so she got a job and saved just about everything she made. With money she received for her birthday and at Christmas, she was able to pay for the trip and have almost $1000 spending money. She did really well and had a great time! She also saved a little money when she decided to go to college. She could have done better at saving for school, but she got too used to buying what she wanted, not just what she needed.

— **P. Thompson**

Show them how to determine if the item they want to purchase is a want or a need. Place the wanted item on a "wanted list" until it becomes a need or is forgotten.

— **J. Wayne King**

Teaching the difference between wants and needs; teaching the value of a good education; giving them responsibility for their own money early in life; teaching them that they are not just going to be given everything they want but should work for what they want.

— **Brenda Bonini**

I try to teach the following: Don't spend what you don't have, live within your means as best you can, and pay off debt as soon as possible.

— **Pamela Barter**

When my children get something they need I now chalk it up as a Christmas or birthday gift. I actually wrap up the note of whatever was bought and expect my children to enthusiastically coo about the surprise. Of course this takes a lot of prompting but it is well worth it.

— **Judy Romanchuk**

Put some money away when you are young, pay down the principle on your mortgage, and try to avoid using credit cards.

— **Randy Payne**

When younger, we let them use their earned allowances to purchase items of need. As they got older my kids all had part-time jobs. (We made sure education came first.) They would help pay for the *luxury* items.

— **Jim Noble**

Let them be responsible for their own finances as much as possible. We try to teach them the value of a dollar and the importance of budgeting. Paying tithing is never optional. We encourage them to save money and have opened savings accounts for them. We try to lead by example by talking as a family about major purchases and by trying to spend wisely. Sometimes we have to say, "Sorry, we just can't afford it right now," or "That purchase is not practical or a good investment."

— **Carla & Mauricio Alpentista**

Help them start saving as early as possible.

— **Carol Arsenault**

Section II

Advanced Power Spending

Chapter 7

Rolling In The Dough

FOOD SAVINGS

"I don't think eating at home more often is saving us any money."

Food, glorious food...it seems we can't go a day without it! We're surrounded by food and obsessed with it. We celebrate with food—holidays, birthdays, anniversaries and weddings. We eat when we're happy or if we're sad; when we're excited and when we're depressed. Sometimes, we even eat food because we are hungry. Whatever the reason for our indulgence...food is a major part of our life and our budget.

In Section I we talked about variable expenses. Food, including groceries, dining out and ordering in, is one of those items in the variable expense category. We have some maneuvering room here. We all have to eat—we just want to help you to eat well for less.

Meal planning

In the 1970s I lived with a German family for three months while I was on a student exchange. We lived in farm country. I walked over to a nearby farm to collect fresh milk from the dairy for our breakfast. Frau Upmann kept a garden and did her grocery shopping for other necessities every day at the grocer's across the street. I suppose she planned her menu based on what was available and looked good that day. The food was always at its freshest and the meals were made from scratch. I don't remember any snacking between meals except for some fruit she kept in a bowl in the hallway. We had breakfast, then a large (hot) meal in the early afternoon and Abendbrot (evening bread—bread and butter, cheese and cold cuts) in the evening. Food shopping and meal preparation were just part of the everyday chores.

Growing up there were always homemade meals. My father kept a large garden and my mother canned and preserved fruits and vegetables. What we didn't have, my mother purchased on her *weekly* grocery shopping trips—time and transportation were important considerations.

In my home today I have to say that there is a lot less "from scratch" cooking than when I was growing up. Many meals I make start from a box, bag or bottle. I look through the weekly grocery flyers for the specials and plan our meals around those foods. I also stock up on items that I regularly use, when they are on sale. Then I always have basic ingredients on hand when I want to make one of my core dishes.

I think I've discovered the hardest part of preparing meals—trying to figure out what to make. I've heard many other people complain about the same thing. There's nothing like standing in your kitchen at 4:30 in the afternoon wondering what you can get onto the dinner table in thirty minutes! If you know ahead of time what you are going to make then half the battle is over.

A friend of mine decided with her husband that they would have set meals every day of the week. It was *Macaroni Monday*, *Pasta Tuesday*, *Fish Wednesday*, *Chicken Thursday*, and *Pizza Friday* at her house each week. She always knew what to pick up at the grocery store, never had to figure out any last minute menus and everyone knew what to expect every day. A little monotonous perhaps but it worked for her family.

Now, we aren't suggesting that you should follow the same regime in your home but we would like you to think about how meal planning can help you. Obviously, our first point has to be that you will save money. You won't have to run out to buy missing ingredients at the convenience store where prices are generally higher. You'll be less tempted to order a pizza when supper needs to be on the table in thirty minutes. Meals you make at home tend to be more nutritious as well. Planning ahead also saves time.

Reduce your preparation time

"American consumers, known to spend upwards of three hours to prepare a meal on weekends, have less than an hour for weekday meals. For many, that's a stretch. Phrases such as pre-cut, pre-washed, ready-to-cook, ready-to-serve, instant, microwaveable and no-time or no-fuss preparation are replacing terms like basting, searing and sauteing in the common vernacular." (Kantha, Shelke. "Food Processing." <u>All Business</u>. 1 August 2005. Web, 8 July 2010 <http://www.allbusiness.com/manufacturing/food-manufacturing/521432-1.html>.)

In our modern society as schedules have become more hectic and the time for meal preparation has been reduced, the food industry has come up with a wide variety of products designed to help us to put our meals together in less time.

Factor This In

Meal planning

Planning meals helps you:

Eat well by varying your food choices throughout the day and week; save time by planning and shopping ahead and reducing trips to the grocery store; and get meals on the table faster with less stress.

Planning tips

Getting started:

1. **Menu plan.** Use a piece of paper, calendar, or a menu planner to jot down your meal ideas.

2. **Grocery list.** Write down the foods you need for the next few days or week.

3. **Go shopping.** Buy the foods you need on your grocery list.

4. **Start cooking.** Post your meal plan on the fridge so whoever gets home first can start the meal.

"Planning Meals." <u>Canada's Food Guide</u>. 5 February 2007. Government of Canada. Web, 8 July 2010 <http://www.hc-sc.gc.ca/fn-an/food-guide-aliment/using-utiliser/plan-eng.php>.

Americans are looking for quick and easy meals and many have turned to these products:

- prepared salads

- pre-cut fresh or frozen veggies and fruits

- meal kits

- prepared entrees

- microwaveable meals

- slow cooker meals

- packaged side dishes

- frozen, precooked portioned meats

These items don't come without a cost of course (two to three times the cost). You save on food preparation time but it will cost you more at the cash register.

Additives

Manufacturers have to make their product last—that's why there's a long list of ingredients on the side of the package.

"Americans spend about ninety percent of their food budget on processed foods, which, unlike whole foods, have been treated in some way after being harvested or butchered. Almost all of these processed foods contain additives, substances intended to change the food in some way before it is sold to consumers. Additives include flavorings that change a food's taste, preservatives that extend its shelf life, colorings that change the way it looks, and dietary additives, such as vitamins, minerals, fatty acids and other supplements…The Food and Drug Administration (FDA) currently has approved more than 3,000 food additives for use in the United States." ("Additives." Sustainable Table. September 2009. Web, 8 July 2010 <http://www.sustainabletable.org/issues/additives/>.)

These are some of the additives you will find listed on packages of food: "acidity regulators, anti-caking agents, anti-foaming agents, antioxidants, bulking agents, colorings, color retention agents, emulsifiers, flavors, flavor enhancers, flour treatment agents, food acids, humectants, preservatives, propellants, stabilizers, sweeteners, artificial sweeteners and thickeners—for food." ("List Of Food Additive Types." Wikipedia, The Free Encyclopedia. Wikimedia Foundation, Inc. 23 June 2010. Web, 8 July 2010 <http://en.wikipedia.org/wiki/List_of_food_additives>.)

You may be concerned about those 3,000 food additives that might show up in your food, but you are pressed for time. Your family wants food on the table, and they want it now! However, if that last paragraph made you feel nervous, you may want to think about alternatives to purchasing store bought products for faster meal preparation. What can you do?

Here are a few suggestions: how about cooking in bulk, participating in meal exchanges or becoming part of a meal group? These ideas may seem to be more about saving time than money, but if they stop the fast food pick-ups and expensive dining out routines, they are about saving money after all.

We've got some tips for bulk cooking in our sidebars and in the additional resources section for you to check out.

How to start a meal exchange

How about joining, or forming, a group to exchange meals? Here's a how-to from a member of one of these groups: "Recently, several couples in our community started a frozen meal exchange. It's a really simple idea. On a certain day, everyone in the exchange meets for coffee and brings along a laundry basket full of frozen meals, one for each family, along with any needed instructions taped to the lid. The members of the club just swap the meals so that everyone takes home one of each meal that they didn't prepare.

It's a very clever idea for several reasons. First, it makes it very easy for people to prepare a variety of home cooked meals. Second, it drastically reduces the meal preparation time, since there's only one big session of making several copies of one meal and after that one only needs to pull a meal out of the freezer and toss it in the oven. Third, it's much cheaper since you can buy the ingredients for your meal in bulk.

A meal exchange is a really great idea to cut down your food costs and your food preparation time without giving up meal variety. If you have a wide social circle, consider starting one up." (Hamm, Trent. "How To Start A Meal Exchange." The Simple Dollar. 23 November 2009. Web, 18 June 2010 <http://www.thesimpledollar.com/2009/11/23/how-to-start-a-meal-exchange/>.)

If you can't find willing participants to form your own meal exchange group, how about...

Makes Cents

Cut your grocery bills in half

1. Learn the art of couponing.

2. Compare apples to apples.

3. Gain leverage from sales flyers.

4. Be a proud card-carrying member.

5. Savor store brand savings.

6. Refuse to be overcharged.

7. Enjoy delayed gratification.

8. Stick to your strategy and avoid the tactics.

Prosser, Faye. "Cut Your Grocery Bills In Half." Family Corner. 2005. Web, 8 July 2010 <http://www.familycorner.com/family/frugal/grocery_bills.shtml>.

Common Cents

"Only when the last tree has died and the last river been poisoned and the last fish been caught will we realize we cannot eat money."

- **Cree Indian Proverb**

Meal assembly groups

Meal assembly kitchens take the hassle out of *home cooked*. The kitchen provides the ingredients and the assembly stations and does the clean-up. This might be a good solution for families on the go. Customers order the number of meals they would like to make. They schedule a session to put the ingredients together according to recipes provided and then store them in freezer bags. The meals are frozen at home and pulled out later when they want a quick meal.

If this idea appeals to you but you are really pressed for time you can have the entrees put together for you and delivered to your home. Each entree will feed 4-6 people and they cost between $15-$30/meal. (If you google "Meal Assembly Kitchen" you can find the nearest store location.)

Online grocery shopping

If this is all too much and you just need something to make things a little easier but you still are prepared to do your own cooking, you can order your groceries online and have them delivered to your home. Saves time but also money if it keeps you away from the fast food drive-thru on your way home from work! (We know, we know, we've said it before...but it's so true!)

Make food go farther

The meal is over and it's time to put the leftovers away. Is it "Oh no! What will I do with that?" or is it an opportunity to come up with another mouth-watering meal? Will that container of leftover rice become another "science project" lost in the back of your fridge or will it become an ingredient in a different meal tomorrow? What if you actually planned to use your leftovers *before* they became leftovers? You cook today knowing that you will eat today and tomorrow. Using leftovers will save time and money and of course reduce waste. The Poulins started using the term "encore meal" to make it sound more attractive than *leftovers*—everyone wants an encore.

Personally, we like turning the leftover roast beef from our Sunday meal into hot roast beef sandwiches the next day, and we like frying up extra hamburger so we can have spaghetti and sauce now and Shepherd's Pie tomorrow and we really like leftover boiled potatoes that turn into fried potatoes for a quick meal when we are pressed for time, and how about....You see what we're saying. Look for more ideas in our additional resources section for how to create "encore" meals!

Grocery shopping

Store selling tactics and how to defend yourself

We all need to eat. Grocers provide food and drink to meet that need—they provide a service. However, they are also in the business of making money and over the years they have learned a few tricks of the trade to increase their sales.

Penny: I feel like I always come out of the grocery store with a lot more than I intended to buy.

Author: You're not alone. Grocers are in the business of making money and they are good at it. Think about these things: Most grocery stores will have the smell of freshly baked goods wafting through the air. Good smells trigger hunger—which in turn tends to make us want to buy more. Don't come hungry.

Grocery stores are set up so that you have to travel through to the back corners of the store for the basics. The longer they can keep you in the store, the more likely you are to spend money. Try to keep your shopping to once a week and stick to your list.

More expensive items, or the brand the store wants you to purchase, are kept at eye level so look above and below for better value. Red and yellow are label colors that attract shoppers' attention. Just because you notice it doesn't mean you have to buy it!

If you aren't careful, you may end up with a few extra items in your grocery cart, and that means a higher grocery bill when you finally get through the checkout line. Does any of that ring a bell?

Penny: It sure does. I guess I'll have to pay more attention when I shop.

Buyer Beware

Grocery stores appeal to your senses

Smell: Probably one of the first things you'll notice when you walk in the store is the smell of baked goods. Mmmm, it smells so good that we feel hungry and when we are hungry, we spend.

Sound: In the background you'll hear music and it's not heavy metal! Those feel-good songs help you to relax and put you in the mood to shop.

Taste: Remember those smells we mentioned? If you head towards the bakery, you just might find something to nibble on. Maybe there's also a little sampling going on elsewhere in the store. Companies like you to try their new products with the hope that you will want to buy them.

Sight: There are beautiful displays all over the store, and always at the ends of the aisles, designed to catch your attention. The goal is that you will "stop, look and buy."

And the checkout station has all those goodies you managed to avoid on your trip around the store—the candies, chocolate bars, magazines, sodas, mints and gum.

Touch: The produce section of the store is definitely a "hands on" experience. There is literally a world of produce at your fingertips. You can tap and squeeze to your heart's content.

Enjoy, but don't let your senses get the better of you!

Sale signs are bright and in your face to make sure you see them. Marketers are also interested in having your children see the signs. (FYI—the most targeted aisle is the cereal aisle; they are enlisting your children's help to make their sales. We consider the perimeter of the grocery store a *safety zone.*)

The sale may be a good deal if you actually need and want that particular item. Also check the end price (the price after the discount), not just the discount amount on an item. Even with the discount, it still may be more than you would normally spend.

Sometimes packaging may give the appearance of more product, when it's just more packaging. It may not be accurate to judge on size alone. Check the weight and the unit price to get a better comparison. Sometimes smaller is better.

When you are standing in the checkout line, you will notice a variety of products set out for your impulse buying enjoyment. If you pick a less busy time to shop—not the weekend and not evenings right after work lets out—you will spend less time in line and be less tempted by these displays.

Shopping tips

Here are some suggestions for a better (more cost effective) shopping experience.

Plan: Write down items that you run out of (or are running short of) during the week. I keep a list on the side of the fridge. When you plan your weekly menus you can add items to your list. Check store flyers when making your meal plans. Check your fridge, pantry, and freezer to make sure you don't buy ingredients you already have. (If you are very organized you can keep lists of the items that you have—one mark for each item— and stroke through the mark when you use an item to keep an accurate count.) If you are aware of items that are getting low, you are better able to watch for them to go on sale. Use the list when you shop and stick to it! You'll keep your costs down and avoid having to make extra trips to the grocery store during the week, or worse, the convenience store on the corner. Plan your shopping route to reduce gas costs if you are going to more than one store. It doesn't make sense to spend $5 on gas to save $2 on a special.

Prepare: Make sure you're not hungry when you shop—reason and common sense can go out the window when everything looks and smells so good!! You may find that leaving the kids at home will save money as well or be prepared to say no about 150 million times. (We may be exaggerating slightly—it may just *feel* like you say it that many times!)

You know you have a budget so you will have to have some system to keep track of what you're spending. You can bring a calculator, or use the calculator function on your cell phone or any other electronic gadget, or just round off the numbers to keep a running total on paper or in your head.

Spend: Keep your kitchen stocked with basic ingredients so that you always have options for quick meals. Buy in bulk when it brings the unit price down or when items are on sale and you will be able to use it up before it expires. Buy fresh veggies and fruit in season to take advantage of cheaper prices. You can even can or freeze them for future use. Frozen veggies and fruit will last longer. Introduce some meatless meals into your menu to cut down on buying expensive meats. Try generic or store brands. Remember that there may be better deals on the bottom shelves of the grocery store. Use coupons but just for items that you need and will use. Comparison shop by looking at unit prices—most stores break it down for you so you don't have to figure it out in your head. Keep an eye on the scanner to watch for incorrect prices when the cashier rings you through.

Save: Make your own bag lunch and snacks—for you and the kids. Make sure you use up what's in your fridge. Leftovers can be used for lunches the next day. You can preplan meals to use up your leftovers. Junk food and sugar cereals are a high price for low nutritional value. Whole foods are cheaper, have higher fiber and nutritional value and are more filling; everything that processed foods are not! Water bottles are passé—opt for a water filter and save the planet! Avoid takeout, delivery and restaurant meals except for special occasions.

Coupons

Using coupons when you shop can save you money. If you want to really save, then you must be prepared to spend some time at it and if you don't want to drive yourself and all the family crazy, you must get organized.

Anyway, here's a few things to think about before you go madly clipping your way through the paper:

- Only use coupons for products that you will use and for things that you need. (Duh—okay, but I've done it before!)

- Your best savings for a $ off coupon will be on the purchase of the smallest size of the product.

- If you bring coupons for several brands of one product then you can use the coupon on the brand that offers the best value.

Right On The Money

What is money?

At first sight the answer to this question seems obvious; the man or woman in the street would agree on coins and banknotes, but would they accept them from any country? What about cheques? They would probably be less willing to accept them than their own country's coins and notes but bank money (i.e. anything for which you can write a cheque) actually accounts for by far the greatest proportion by value of the total supply of money. What about I.O.U.s (I owe you), credit cards and gold? The gold standard belongs to history but even today many rich people in different parts of the world would rather keep some of their wealth in the form of gold than in official, inflation-prone currencies....

All sorts of things have been used as money at different times in different places. The alphabetical list below, taken from page 27 of *A History of Money* by Glyn Davies, includes but a minute proportion of the enormous variety of primitive moneys, and none of the modern forms: amber, beads, cowries, drums, eggs, feathers, gongs, hoes, ivory, jade, kettles, leather, mats, nails, oxen, pigs, quartz, rice, salt, thimbles, umiacs, vodka, wampum, yarns, and zappozats (decorated axes).

Davies, Roy. "Origins Of Money And Of Banking." Project Exeter. 25 May 2005. Web, 8 July 2010 <http://projects.exeter.ac.uk/RDavies/arian/origins.html>.

Bank On It

Get your grocery coupons organized

Clipping coupons

Timing— Try to choose the same day and time to clip your grocery coupons each week.

Method—Now when it comes to clipping your free grocery coupons you have several methods to choose from....

- Clip them all out.

- Clip out only the coupons you know you will use.

- Don't clip out any of the coupons, but save them in their whole page form.

Storing coupons

Inexpensive containers

- gallon size plastic zip bags

- recycled envelopes

- small baskets

- 4x6 file boxes

- recycled shoeboxes, diaper wipe containers or empty food boxes

Index Dividers

- [Use] store bought dividers or [make] your own dividers.

- [Label] your dividers.

Jones, Michelle. "Living A Better Life." Better Budgeting. Web, 28 July 2010 <http://www.betterbudgeting.com/articles/frugal/couponqueen.htm>.

- If you shop at a store that doubles or triples coupons you will usually save more. If a store doesn't offer double coupons but has lower prices than the store you usually use, we think you know what you should do.

- If you come prepared with all your coupons you may be able to take advantage of a store special that you weren't expecting. A sale may be good; a sale with coupons is better.

- Make sure using the coupon will actually save you money and enough that it gives you better value. When you are required to buy more than one item to use the coupon, you need to divide your coupon amount by the number of items. Is the deal still good? What if a perfectly good generic brand still costs less than the name brand even with the coupon discount. You aren't obligated to use the coupon. It's about getting good value.

Buying in bulk

It's great to buy in bulk if it saves you time and money down the road, but you don't want to find out later that you wasted your money.

Here are some things to consider before you go out and do that big shop:

- When you bring your purchases home will you have enough room to store them all?

- Is your freezer large enough to store everything *before* and *after* you cook?

- If you buy large quantities of a particular item, will your family eat it?

It doesn't matter if the price was good if no one likes it or if it expires before it can be eaten.

You may want to try one can, box or bag of a new item first before you buy larger quantities of it to make sure that you and your family will enjoy the taste. It's better to find out that you don't like it when it costs you $1, than when you've spent $10.

If you bulk purchase and stock up on super sales, you can build a base of regular food that will last until the next sale. There are sales cycles that you can use to plan for bulk purchases. For example, Robin has noticed that *3 boxes of cereal for $5* sales happen at the end of the first quarter of the year so she buys mega amounts at this time (enough to get through to the next sale) and saves hundreds of dollars. Of course afterwards she reduced her grocery shopping budget accordingly over the next 6 months to account for the large amount spent on the bulk purchase.

Check the expiry dates when you make a purchase and mark it on the package so that it gets used before it expires. If there is no expiry date on the package then mark the date of purchase and use a product shelf life guide to create your own expiry date. Make sure that you rotate items so that older items aren't pushed to the back of the cupboard, pantry, fridge or freezer and forgotten. Remember, if you save money on the purchase, but don't use what you have bought, you haven't really saved.

Eating out/dining in

We know that we've just spent most of this chapter convincing you to stay at home and cook for yourself. But, let's face it, it's not reasonable to expect that you will *never* eat out. Certainly, you can and will go out for meals. We all get tired of our own cooking (maybe that's just me) and we like a break.

You can choose to "dine in" at home to reduce the costs of restaurant food. Order the entree—pizza for example—and provide your own drink, salad/veggies and dessert. You get a break from cooking without breaking the bank.

How about a picnic in your living room? Grab a blanket and the plastic dinnerware and even sandwiches, fruit and cold soda become a treat. You won't have to worry about sand in your food or rainy skies. If the weather is nice, then head outdoors with your picnic basket—even if it's just to the backyard or your local park. The fresh air will do you good.

Makes Cents

Tips for successful freezer foods

There are different methods for freezing food that you may use depending upon what you have cooked.

- freezer bags

- foil and plastic

- vacuum sealer

Label all the food that you put in the freezer....Use post it notes (with extra tape) on the outside of each item or a Sharpie pen....Write what the meal is and the cooking instructions.

Freezer Tips:

- Cool food before freezing.

- Put the date on the meal so you know when it was frozen.

- Wipe edges of containers clean.

- Frozen cooked meat and poultry in sauces will keep 5-6 months.

- Sauces and soups will keep 5-6 months.

- Freeze as flat and thin as possible to make stacking in the freezer much easier. [This also makes defrosting the meal much faster as well.]

Anderson, Candace. "Learn Once A Month Cooking In 7 Easy Steps." Frugal Mom. 22 May 2010. Web, 8 July 2010 <http://www.frugalmom.net/blog/2010/05/7-steps-to-once-a-monthcooking/>.

Your Money's Worth

Money saving ideas for eating out

What's a restaurant junkie to do? Here are a few tips that might help ease the pain.

1. **Check local publications for coupons.** Local newspapers... often run coupons from local restaurants. Consider the 50 cents [cost for the newspaper] as a good ROI for nabbing a 2-for-1 or $-off coupon.

2. **Dine during happy hour or late at night.** Most restaurants offer specials during hours that aren't normally busy—yeah, who wants to eat at 5 or 10 p.m. but a deal is a deal.

3. **Stick with the appetizer or starter section of the menu.** Sure the portions are smaller than entrees, but would it kill us to eat a little lighter? Sometimes the most interesting items are tucked away here anyway.

4. **Share an entree.** Most entrees are big enough for at least 1 ½ portions or even two. A small house salad and half an entree generally satisfies most people.... This is an easy way to self-impose portion control.

5. **Dine in small, independently owned ethnic restaurants.** Most often, the food is inexpensive yet packed with vibrant, exciting flavors. And it gives us an opportunity to explore another cuisine.

Adapted from: Walters, Gwen Ashley. "5 Money Saving Tips For Dining Out." Pen & Fork. 16 September 2009. Web, 8 July 2010 <http://penandfork.wordpress.com/2009/09/16/5-money-saving-tips-for-dining-out/>.

Bill: That's okay but sometimes I just want to go out to a restaurant. Any suggestions?

Author: There are ways to save money when eating out. Look for coupons in the paper or on the Internet for your favorite restaurants. Also, buffet-style places can give you big variety at a reasonable price.

Be flexible. Lunch menus often offer lower-priced meals as compared to supper menus. Look for the restaurant "specials," their lower-priced entrees. Many restaurants offer "kids eat free" nights during the week.

Watch the small things that add up quickly, those little extras that don't come with the meal. You can save a large amount on your bill by drinking water.

Most of us don't need an entree and an appetizer. You can skip the appetizer or share one with a friend. Some menus offer smaller portion (smaller price) meals—which by the way are more likely to be the recommended serving size. Serving sizes have grown—if you don't want to grow along with them then share an entree with a friend.

Bill: Okay, I can make a few changes...that's not so hard.

Author: Just one last suggestion: Even though the desserts are very tempting, they can be pricey. Why not pick up a lower-priced dessert on the way home or plan for a nice dessert at home? (And, as Robin reminded me, dinner can end without a dessert—okay, party pooper.)

A little planning, organization and creativity can save you a lot of money. Use these meal planning, grocery shopping and eating out tips to increase your enjoyment and lower your costs.

We make these suggestions:

- Save time, money and headaches by meal planning.

- Free up time with bulk cooking, meal exchanges, assembly groups, and online shopping.

- Lower grocery costs by buying in bulk, using coupons and shopping smart.

- Defend yourself from marketing ploys.

- Enjoy your meal out and make sure the price is right.

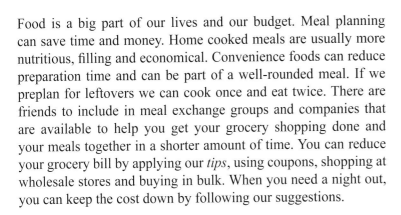

Food is a big part of our lives and our budget. Meal planning can save time and money. Home cooked meals are usually more nutritious, filling and economical. Convenience foods can reduce preparation time and can be part of a well-rounded meal. If we preplan for leftovers we can cook once and eat twice. There are friends to include in meal exchange groups and companies that are available to help you get your grocery shopping done and your meals together in a shorter amount of time. You can reduce your grocery bill by applying our *tips*, using coupons, shopping at wholesale stores and buying in bulk. When you need a night out, you can keep the cost down by following our suggestions.

So, with a good meal under our belts we are ready to venture into the world of entertainment...break a leg!!

Fool's Gold

Top 5 most expensive restaurants in the world

1. **Aragawa—Tokyo**
   The first steakhouse in Japan hasn't failed to satisfy the taste buds of customers. (For just a steak...) Dinner for one: $368

2. **Alain Ducasse au Plaza Athénée—Paris**
   Located on the very chic Avenue Montaigne, this gourmet restaurant is at the same time very trendy and elegant, stylish and modern. Dinner for one: $231.

3. **Gordon Ramsay—London**
   Gordon Ramsay a British chef made his venture into the field of restaurant business with his eponymous restaurant in 1998....Cornish Lamb and pigeon with foie gras are the mainstay features of the menu. Dinner for one: $183.

4. **Acquarello—Munich**
   The Acquarello is without a doubt the number one Italian restaurant in Munich....Acquarello transports its guests to the world of Italian cuisine beyond pizza and chianti. Dinner for one: $125.

5. **Alberto Ciarla—Rome**
   Alberto Ciarla's Trastevere fish restaurant is a historic landmark on Rome's gastronomic map. The décor is a time warp of 1970s glamour, and the food is spectacular in a more tasteful sense. Dinner for one: $113.

Adapted from: "Top 5 Most Expensive Restaurant In The World." Crazy Junkyard. 1 July 2009. Web, 23 July 2010 <http://www.crazyjunkyard.com/top-5-most-expensive-restaurants-in-the-world/>.

Web sites used in the chapter

http://bit.ly/bXjr9c	(LearnersDictionary.com) A definition of "roll."
http://bit.ly/as5nLD	(Wikipedia) A definition of "bread."
http://bit.ly/c30lKv	(AllBusiness.com) How we use shortcuts to make a "home cooked meal" in less time.
http://bit.ly/bwYxi6	(Health Canada) Canada's food guide and meal planning.
http://bit.ly/bgukuY	(SustainableTable.org) "Food Additives."
http://bit.ly/b9t1bx	(MommysIdeaBook.com) "13 Ways To Save Time In The Kitchen."
http://bit.ly/b34A02	(Wikipedia) "List Of Food Additive Types."
http://bit.ly/dxEgT3	(TheSimpleDollar.com) "How To Start A Meal Exchange."
http://bit.ly/arynMp	(FamilyCorner.com) 8 essential techniques to cut grocery bills in half.
http://bit.ly/nbjSb	(Tipnut.com) "Once A Month Cooking: Tips & Resources."
http://bit.ly/bxSJah	(SavingsNut.com) "Grocery Money Saving And Budgeting Tips."
http://bit.ly/abd6s3	(Exeter.ac.uk) "Origins Of Money And Of Banking."
http://bit.ly/1ts2jC	(Better Budgeting) "Get Your Grocery Coupons Organized!"
http://bit.ly/aUkJBz	(FrugalMom.net) 7 steps to once a month cooking.
http://bit.ly/977elu	(Pen & Fork) "5 Money Saving Tips For Dining Out."
http://bit.ly/d7o6BS	(CrazyJunkyard.com) "Top 5 Most Expensive Restaurants In The World."

Additional resources

Meal planning

http://bit.ly/92UmZM	(BulkFreezerCooking.com) All things related to bulk cooking, freezer cooking and canning.
http://bit.ly/bGE0MZ	(Freezer Friends) An example of a meal exchange group.
http://bit.ly/chsgic	(HowStuffWorks.com) Cook once, eat twice meal ideas.

Grocery shopping

http://bit.ly/dvvHBE	(ZenHabits.net) 50 tips for Grocery Shopping.
http://bit.ly/d5PNHk	(Canada) (Flyerland.ca) Get flyers online localized to your city.
http://bit.ly/9Ja5hI	(USA) (TheGroceryGame.com) Save $100 on your grocery bill each month with coupons.

Eating out/dining in

http://bit.ly/coAEEL	(Woman's Day) "Money Saving Ideas For Dining Out."
http://bit.ly/cgJ9SR	(Helium.com) 41 articles on how to save money dining out.
http://bit.ly/aywXoo	(USA) (Restaurant.com) Best deals and discounts on local restaurants.

We asked, "How do you keep food/grocery costs down?" and you said...

Things like ready-made soups in a can, or box dinners, can be made to stretch by adding more noodles or rice. One soup package with some browned onions, peppers, a can of crushed tomatoes and some leftover pasta can make that soup go a long way. Rice-a-roni with browned onions and peppers, chicken or ham chunks, and veggies makes one box into a meal for the whole family. Simply adding leftovers to these types of meals eliminates waste and makes a small inexpensive box stretch into a meal.

— **Mary Dubeau**

Watch the flyers—stock up when items are on sale.

— **April S.**

Shop sales, buy in bulk, use less meat, and buy less junk food.

— **Andrew Pigou**

Portion control has made about $5 difference per week, and helped me lose weight.

— **Craig Johnson**

I would rather buy more groceries and not go out to eat, and save that way.

— **Akif Srajeldin**

We shop sales and use coupons. We shop at discount stores if we're driving by them. If not, we shop at the grocery store in town as we save money on gas by buying locally.

— **Anna Coutts**

We buy only what we are going to eat. I don't go grocery shopping on an empty stomach.

— **Hector Garcia**

Buy lots when an item is on sale, stick to menus, and use a list. I try to shop on the outside store aisles so I can stay away from processed foods.

— **Darla Bradley**

I make a list before grocery shopping and only allow four purchases of items not on the list.

— **Adam Norwick**

Go vegetarian! Cook from scratch. Have a series of few meals that use similar ingredients (especially if there is only one or two of you in the house) so that you can buy those items in bulk without getting tired of them. Buy seasonal produce, and learn to cook inexpensive vegetables like cabbage and rutabagas in ways you enjoy.

— **Kirsten Nelson**

Buy in bulk, especially when items are on sale.

— **Lisa Sedore**

Stock up on sale items and shop around.

— **Rhonda Dubeau**

Bulk shopping.

— **Mike Kucey**

I try to buy where I see the best sales in the flyers.

— **Nicole Westcott**

I'm never too tired to cook, but sometimes I might get a frozen dinner. My main dishes are fish or chicken—rarely steak, occasionally a roast beef dinner.

— **Laura Gordon**

Your quick and easy meal ideas:

• mac & cheese	• nachos	• homemade pizza	• french fries
• french toast	• pancakes	• burgers	• TV dinner
• soup	• stew	• stir-fry	• wraps
• sandwiches	• slow cooker meals	• waffles	• brown beans/toast
• spaghetti	• eggs	• tuna melt	• grilled cheese
• tacos	• chili	• cereal	• salads

For more ideas from people just like you, visit http://powerspendingbook.com/by-the-people

P.S. A few comments "by the people."

Chapter 8

Fun On A Shoestring Budget

SAVING ON LEISURE AND ENTERTAINMENT

Seniors Dance

7:00 p.m. - **9:00** p.m.

TICKETS

FREE

"I need a night out, and the price is right!"

There's always so much to do in a day. You've worked hard and it's time to relax. In fact, we think that you *deserve a break* —a little *R & R*—some *down time*. Is there anything we North Americans enjoy more than our leisure time? Apparently, on an average day, (besides sleep) the only thing we do more than work is play. And since people want to eat, have shelter and wear clothes we can understand why work comes first. Though "all play, and no work, makes Jack a mere toy," remember that "all work, and no play, makes Jack a dull boy." We don't want to be accused of being dull now do we? So, it's time to explore the world of leisure and entertainment.

Leisure time

Leisure can be divided into two categories: active and passive. As you might expect, active leisure requires some use of physical or mental energy. Passive leisure activities don't.

The US Census Bureau reports the top ten *leisure* activities of Americans in 2009: dining out, reading, entertaining friends or relatives at home, barbequing, going to the beach, baking, cooking for fun, playing cards, playing PC/computer games and going to bars/nightclubs. (Note the absence of social media activities above but we expect that it won't be long before they make the top of the list!) You'll notice that though these activities are fun and relaxing they don't exactly get the heart pumping.

Physical activity is also fun and relaxing but offers many health benefits and so it is important to incorporate activity into your everyday life. That will be our focus in this chapter. We want to show you how to do that without costing an arm and a leg. (That would be self-defeating, wouldn't it?)

So, though at first talking about physical activity may not seem to relate to saving money, it certainly does relate to your quality of life. And if we consider the rising cost of healthcare, anything we can do personally to prevent injury, illness and reduce stress will reduce our own medical costs and hopefully the taxes we pay to cover health care costs. But perhaps you will say to us, "I can't afford to go to a gym," or "I have no room for exercise equipment in my house." The good news is that there are LOTS of ways for you and your family to get active that cost little or no money and don't take up space in your living room, garage or basement.

Penny: I know I should be more active but besides the cost I wonder where I'll find the time. I always seem to be busy and then at the end of the day I'm too tired.

Author: There's no doubt about it. Life can be hectic. So, look for opportunities to sneak a little more exercise into your day. You can exercise in small time frames—10 minutes at a time 3/day—instead of 30 minute sessions. Take a walk around the block or around the office building at lunch. Climbing stairs is better exercise than taking the elevator and you won't have to stand around waiting for the elevator to arrive. Park a little farther away than you need to and get a few extra steps into your day.

Even housework can become an opportunity instead of a chore. Any activity burns calories—your body doesn't know if you are dancing or vacuuming. I was never so enthusiastic about shoveling my driveway as when I heard that I could burn up to 600 calories/hour. Give me that shovel!!

Penny: Makes you look at housework in a whole new way, doesn't it?

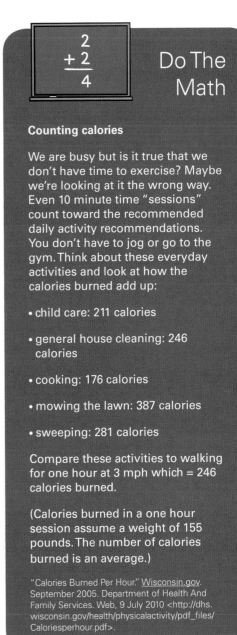

Do The Math

Counting calories

We are busy but is it true that we don't have time to exercise? Maybe we're looking at it the wrong way. Even 10 minute time "sessions" count toward the recommended daily activity recommendations. You don't have to jog or go to the gym. Think about these everyday activities and look at how the calories burned add up:

- child care: 211 calories

- general house cleaning: 246 calories

- cooking: 176 calories

- mowing the lawn: 387 calories

- sweeping: 281 calories

Compare these activities to walking for one hour at 3 mph which = 246 calories burned.

(Calories burned in a one hour session assume a weight of 155 pounds. The number of calories burned is an average.)

"Calories Burned Per Hour." Wisconsin.gov. September 2005. Department of Health And Family Services. Web, 9 July 2010 <http://dhs. wisconsin.gov/health/physicalactivity/pdf_files/ Caloriesperhour.pdf>.

Low-cost ways to be active

When you are ready to increase the time you spend exercising, walking is one of the cheapest, safest and easiest exercises around. If weather is a problem, there are indoor tracks or you can walk at the mall—weather problem solved. It may make it easier to stay committed to an exercise program if you join a walking group or find a buddy and set a walking schedule. It's harder to stay on the couch when you know someone is counting on you.

If you are willing to spend a little on exercise products to help you reach your fitness goals, consider these low-cost accessories: dumbbells, resistance tubing, skipping ropes, exercise videos/ DVDs (I pick them up at secondhand stores). If you're willing to spend a little more, and if your kids have a game system already, you can pick up a fitness video game.

You probably have things in your home right now that you can use in your exercise routine. Canned soup makes a great hand-held weight and step stools can be used for step training. You can even purposely make extra trips up and down your stairs to get in some *real* stair climbing exercise.

There may be fitness resources available at your local high school or at a nearby community center that offer lower fees (than a gym) to use their equipment. Your tax dollars are already paying for the facility so community members are given a financial break when using the resources: swimming pools, squash and tennis courts, and fitness centers. They may also offer fitness and aerobic classes.

If you want exercise equipment you can probably find it online, in the classifieds, at yard sales and in used equipment stores—might as well let someone else take the initial financial hit. Ask your family and friends first—they may have equipment (taking up space) that they'd like to get rid of. You get equipment and they get some cash and everybody wins. Do some research on the equipment before you purchase it to make sure that you don't get stuck with a "lemon" or something you will never use. You might be able to share some costs with a friend, like sharing personal training sessions or purchasing exercise DVDs that you can exchange with each other so you don't get bored with the same old routine.

If you have any concerns about your fitness level, or if it's been a while since you've seen your doctor, schedule an appointment and get your doctor's approval before starting an exercise program. Then start slowly, but do start.

In the family way

When you are at home with your family, including physical activity is about setting a good example, getting every *body* moving and having fun. Need some ideas? Think about what you did as a kid. Even on rainy days we found ways to amuse ourselves. We weren't sitting in front of the television or computer screen and we didn't have a hand-held device to amuse us either. Introduce these ideas to your children and grandchildren and join in the fun.

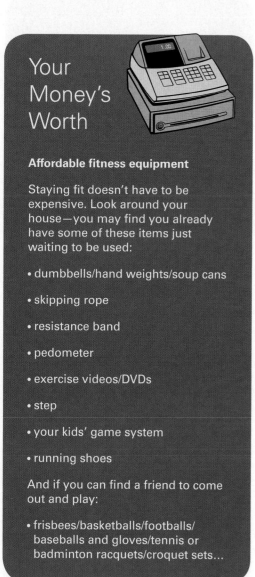

Your Money's Worth

Affordable fitness equipment

Staying fit doesn't have to be expensive. Look around your house—you may find you already have some of these items just waiting to be used:

• dumbbells/hand weights/soup cans

• skipping rope

• resistance band

• pedometer

• exercise videos/DVDs

• step

• your kids' game system

• running shoes

And if you can find a friend to come out and play:

• frisbees/basketballs/footballs/ baseballs and gloves/tennis or badminton racquets/croquet sets...

Here are a few ideas from my childhood: We built an indoor fort out of blankets and chairs and used boxes to build a puppet play theater or a kitchen play set. We spent a lot of time choreographing favorite songs (we were so cool in our hot pants and high heeled boots!) and playing dress-up. We played charades and role plays, and it cost NOTHING.

You can set up a bowling alley in the basement with a ball and some juice cartons, or have a small basketball net for more indoor fun. If your basement is large enough you can rollerblade, or play hockey and soccer games.

Of course, we want to get outside when we can. There are lots of things to do in your own backyard! Jump rope, play hopscotch or kickball. Play family baseball, soccer or basketball. You can create an obstacle course or hold your own "wacky" Olympics. Play "tag," "hide and seek," "Simon says" or "red light, green light." We had regular games of "kick the can." Everyone loves blowing bubbles. Kids love to chase them and break them before they float away! Play in the sprinkler. We've made our own "slip and slide" at a very low cost. If you are blessed with winter snow you can set up a backyard rink, build a snow fort, make a snowman or a snow angel.

Take your family bicycling or rollerblading around the neighborhood. Talk is cheap and so is walking—your dog (or your neighbor's dog) can never get enough and the added bonus is time to talk as a couple or parent to child, away from the TV and telephone. You might even be able to turn dog walking into a small business—exercise *and* money—it'll *pay* to exercise!

Everybody has a park nearby with free equipment and if you walk to and from it you'll burn extra calories. Organize a neighborhood scavenger hunt. Go swimming at a beach or local pool. We all need physical activity every day. Stay fit and have fun as a family!!

Entertain me(nt)

Entertainment again is a use of our leisure time but is less about *doing and participating* and more about *observing*. Entertainment is about amusement and diversion and is generally a passive activity.

Right On The Money

The cost of entertainment

You probably spend more on entertainment than you do on groceries, clothing or gasoline.

If you don't believe it, take a few minutes to total your monthly costs, starting with the services that have you locked in: basic cable television, and any premium channels, like HBO or Showtime; Netflix to rent videos; TiVo for digital recording; your high-speed Internet connection; and perhaps, satellite radio and streaming music like Yahoo Music. You are already up to about $200 a month, or $2,400 a year.

Don't forget your iTunes music and video downloads, plus magazines, movie rentals, movie tickets, live shows and sporting events.

Add in your cell phone and any of its video, data and premium content.

The average American spends more on entertainment than on gasoline, household furnishings and clothing and nearly the same amount as spent on dining out, according to the Bureau of Labor Statistics.

Darlin, Damon. "How To Tame An Inflated Entertainment Budget." The New York Times. 19 November 2005. Web, 9 July 2010 <http://www.nytimes.com/2005/11/19/business/19money.html?_r=1>.

Makes Cents

Quick ideas for cheap dates

1. [Go on a] picnic.

2. Lie on a hill, spot cloud shapes.

3. Find shells at the beach.

4. Play board games.

5. [Take a] scenic drive in the country.

6. [Visit an] art gallery.

7. [Go to the] free museum night.

8. Find vintage stuff at garage sales.

9. [Attend] amateur night at a comedy club.

10. Play with animals at a pet shop.

11. Check out a local band.

12. [Visit an] art fair.

13. [Do a] crossword puzzle in the park.

14. Test drive cars.

15. [Attend a] swap meet.

16. Attend a book reading.

17. [Take a] local factory tour.

18. [Go] house hunting.

19. Go to the mall.

This list was provided by HotDateIdeas.com and can be found on the website along with other great ideas.
"Quick Ideas For Cheap Dates." Hot Date Ideas. Ed. David Hall. Web, 15 March 2010 <http://www.hotdateideas.com/cheap-date-ideas#cheapQuick #cheapQuick>.

When we are entertained someone else does the work while we sit back and enjoy the show. However, we are going to broaden our use of the word *entertainment* in this section to refer to activities that may be passive or active but that serve a higher purpose—relationship-building. And since "one is the loneliest number" and "two's company" we wanted to explore some inexpensive dating ideas.

It's a date

Courtship and dating have changed over time from arranged marriages and matchmaking to speed dating and dating coaches. We expect our readers are past the teenage years but may perhaps be young enough to still be in the dating stage.

Bill: *Well, obviously this section doesn't apply to me. I'm married...all that dating stuff is behind me.*

Author: **With the divorce rate being what it is who can say for sure just when the dating stage begins and ends? Anyway, in our opinion you are NEVER too old to date; dating doesn't stop with the "I dos." Couples need time to focus on each other and to keep their relationship fresh and strong.**

Bill: *I don't know about this...you know, "been there, done that."*

Author: **Married or not, everyone can enjoy these creative and inexpensive date ideas. Bill, out of hundreds of ideas we will just suggest a few. Trust us—Penny will love it and we think you'll have fun too.**

In fact, we know many couples who schedule a weekly date night. They know how important it is to spend time together—alone. You may want to mark it on your calendar. You know what they say, "Happy wife, happy life."

At home dates—have a movie night and share your favorite childhood movie and a bag of microwave popcorn; challenge your date to a favorite board game; cook your date's favorite meal; play "twenty questions."

Outdoor dates—throw on your bathing suits and wash the car; go sledding; golf in the snow with colored golf balls; go to the drive-in on a warm summer night, bring chairs, pillows and blankets for an under-the-stars experience (but don't forget the bug spray); shoot some hoops together, winner buys dessert.

Away dates—go to a flea market and buy something for each other for $5 or less; go rollerblading; go to an indoor rock climbing gym; go to a local car dealership and take a test drive; visit a chocolate or cookie factory; visit an art gallery or museum; eat a sunrise breakfast picnic; go to an art show.

Romantic dates—have a candlelight picnic in the backyard; take a walk on the beach at sunset or in the moonlight; "dine in" at home and enlist family or friends to be your waiters; spread a blanket on the ground or on the trunk of the car and watch the stars.

Group dates—invite some other couples over for a potluck dinner and/or a games night; have a bubble blowing contest; play balloon badminton or volleyball; have a progressive dinner with several other couples; organize a car rally; have a movie marathon where everyone brings snacks to share; play croquet in the backyard—girls versus guys.

Family time

Remember this little rhyme? "First comes love, then comes marriage, then comes a baby in the baby carriage." What do you do with the little critters once you've got them? Going out as a family can be expensive. We've already talked about some activities that you can participate in with your kids in the last section. We want to talk about a few more.

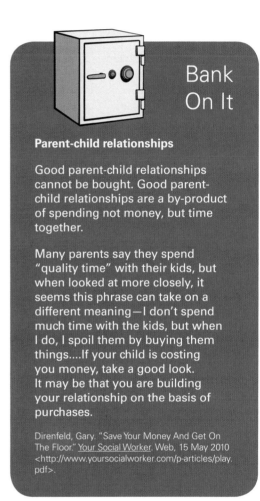

Bank On It

Parent-child relationships

Good parent-child relationships cannot be bought. Good parent-child relationships are a by-product of spending not money, but time together.

Many parents say they spend "quality time" with their kids, but when looked at more closely, it seems this phrase can take on a different meaning—I don't spend much time with the kids, but when I do, I spoil them by buying them things....If your child is costing you money, take a good look. It may be that you are building your relationship on the basis of purchases.

Direnfeld, Gary. "Save Your Money And Get On The Floor." Your Social Worker. Web, 15 May 2010 <http://www.yoursocialworker.com/p-articles/play. pdf>.

Fool's Gold

Rock star extravagances

Beat This—Michael Jackson
Item: Marlon Brando for $1,000,000

Marlon Brando attended Michael Jackson's 30th Anniversary show in September 2001. The actor, a long-time friend of the "King of Pop," was paid one million to attend the concert.

Burger King—Elvis Presley
Purchase: Peanut butter and bacon sandwiches for $3,387

Elvis Presley, while entertaining two Colorado policemen at Graceland, remembered a sandwich he had once eaten at a restaurant in Denver: a hollowed out, buttered loaf, filled with peanut butter, jelly and a pound of fried bacon. When one officer showed some interest in the snack, the King insisted they try it out. So they drove down to Memphis airport ...where his private jet was waiting. Two hours later, they were enjoying 22 of the $49.95 "Fool's Gold" sandwiches on silver platters and a case of champagne....

Florist Fire—Elton John
Purchase: Flowers for $296,000

During a court case in 2000 where he sued his former manager and his accountants, it was revealed that the singer spent a little more than a quarter of a million on flowers between 1996 and 1997. When he was questioned about it during the trial, he replied simply, "I like flowers."

Saldanha, Kenneth. "11 Rock-star Extravagances." Planet Radiocity. Web, 9 July 2010 <http://www.planetradiocity.com/musicreporter/celebrity-features-story.php?featureid=131&title=11%20Rock-Star%20Extravagances>.

One-on-one time

What do our children need from us? They need us to talk to them about our life and about theirs. They need us to play with them and to be there when they play. They need us to listen to them when they want to talk. They just want us to be with them, even at times sitting quietly. They need one-on-one time with each parent because each child is an individual. They need quality time but also quantity of time. One-on-one time doesn't have to break the budget and being frugal will help teach your child that having fun is not dependent on spending money.

How can you make time for your children? You may have scheduled times with each child during the week. You can take a child with you when you run errands. You may designate a day out with each child. Maybe you plan a lunch or dessert at a local fast food restaurant every so often. Or just "grab and go" spontaneously—drive to the beach, walk to the park, read a book together, play a game. You'll have a chance to talk and your child won't have to compete for your attention.

Importance of family time

We also need to spend time together as a family. In the past, one of the most common times for a family to gather together was around the dinner table. Unfortunately, this tradition seems to be missing in many households. Everyone grabs something for himself, eats on the run or in front of the television.

There has been a call in recent years for families to return to the dinner table. "Eating together regularly can be a wonderful source of family time, a way of slowing down and keeping a family in contact during a hectic week...here are some [good reasons to gather your family around the dinner table] and why it is important:

- regular meal times provide stability

- eating together encourages communication

- it relieves stress

- it's just plain fun" (Adapted from: Mooney, Belinda. "The Importance Of Family Meals." Suite 101. 6 July 2007. Web, 9 July 2010 <http://parentingmethods.suite101.com/article.cfm/the_importance_of_family_meals>.)

So when family meal time is over and you are looking for something to do together here are a few suggestions for activities: go to a petting zoo; attend high school plays (they are cheaper than the "real" thing and you support local youth); work on a family puzzle; go fly a kite—literally; rake the leaves together and then jump in them before bagging them up; build a huge sand castle at the beach; go feed the ducks down at the lake; play in the snow or dance in the rain; camp out in the backyard. It doesn't have to cost money to be fun. Your family members just want your time and attention.

In fact, many families are choosing to have family nights. They organize games or movie nights (get free movies from the library), participate in volunteer and community projects, go on an outing like a walk or bike ride or just play outdoor games together. Even a trip to a park in another part of the city can be fun and exciting. They also plan a special treat to share together: they bake and decorate cookies, make their own pizzas or sundaes, eat popcorn balls or some other favorite dessert. Use your imagination. The idea is to have regular, scheduled time together. Pick a night of the week that works for your family.

If you include your children in the discussion, they will have their own ideas of what your family can do together. Kids can find joy in the simplest of activities. They are more interested in just spending time with you. After a while, you may find that they will be willing to help in the planning and preparation of your activities. It won't be long before they will be reminding you that it's time for family night.

Other cost cutting entertainment ideas

There are more ways to cut down on entertainment costs. How about tickets to a dress rehearsal for a play or concert? If your family likes a particular attraction and it's a place that you would go for repeated visits then pay for an annual pass. Places like parks, zoos, science centers, aquariums, planetariums, amusement parks, etc. offer both annual passes and discounted entry fee days. Coupon or entertainment books for your area can offer big discounts on local attractions. (It's only a good purchase if you actually use the coupons and save more than the cost of the book.) DVD/video swaps with friends and family can give you a new set of viewing options for your movie nights instead of having to rent movies. Keep a lookout for previously-enjoyed movies at thrift stores, or even your local video store, if you want to increase your home movie library.

Common Cents

"Hollywood is a place where they'll pay you a thousand dollars for a kiss and fifty cents for your soul."
- **Marilyn Monroe**

"My problem lies in reconciling my gross habits with my net income."
- **Errol Flynn**

"A bank is a place that will lend you money if you can prove that you don't need it."
- **Bob Hope**

"There is only one class in the community that thinks more about money than the rich, and that is the poor. The poor can think of nothing else."
- **Oscar Wilde**

"Lack of money is the root of all evil."
- **George Bernard Shaw**

"Money frees you from doing things you dislike. Since I dislike doing nearly everything, money is handy."
- **Groucho Marx**

Leisure and entertainment are important parts of our culture. Fortunately, there are hundreds of inexpensive (downright cheap) or free leisure and entertainment ideas. Look for low-cost fitness, date ideas and family activities in the additional resources section. We also asked people for their ideas—you'll find these at the end of the chapter. We'd love to add your great ideas as well!

Hobbies into cash

We just want to briefly mention that your leisure time hobbies can become income-producing activities. You may make just enough to cover the costs of purchasing the supplies and equipment for your favorite pasttime—still a bonus because the money isn't coming out of your own pocket anymore. If you are very fortunate, and providing that's your goal, it may even turn into a part- or full-time business for you. I think this is where work is no longer *work*.

We have focused on increasing wealth by reducing our spending and finding ways to lower our costs, but as we've mentioned before, wealth can also be increased by raising our income or by combining the two strategies—spend less, make more. Implementing cost saving strategies can only take us so far; there is a threshold that we cannot go under—we all need food, clothing and shelter, and there are costs associated with obtaining these items.

On the other hand, when we increase our income there is potentially no limit (well, actually the "sky is the limit") to how high our income can go. As long as we don't increase our spending to match our increased earnings, we can build wealth at a faster pace than just by living frugally.

Turning hobbies into cash making activities is one way to supplement income. Consider your other interests, skills and talents—how can you use them to create additional income? If you have something to *sell* there's usually someone willing to *buy*.

We make these suggestions:

- Leisure time is important—passive and active—make use of the time you have.

- Health care is expensive. It's imperative that we manage our health costs by staying active.

- There are low-cost and free ways to stay fit.

- Dating can be inexpensive and fun. There is no age limit and it shouldn't end after you are married.

- It's important to spend time together as a family and it doesn't have to cost a lot, if anything at all.

- You may be able to "cash in" on your hobbies.

We've discussed the importance of leisure and entertainment. We've talked about passive leisure like watching TV, playing cards or dining out. We've also looked at active leisure activities like walking, biking and swimming. Keeping active and staying fit is important and it doesn't have to cost us any, or much, money. We can involve our entire family in a healthy lifestyle.

Entertainment provides diversion and amusement and is usually passive, but not always (at least not under our definition). There are hundreds of inexpensive ideas for couple and group dates. When you want to spend time with your family you can choose from a wide variety of activities at home, in your own backyard or away from home. You can take advantage of money saving ideas for more traditional activities as well.

We hope you've been *entertained*—that was our goal. Now we believe we're ready to venture a little further afield—grab your luggage and let's go…

Money Talks

A shoestring budget

Meaning

Life on a shoestring budget, travel on a shoestring budget, food on a shoestring budget…apparently *anything* can be on a shoestring budget.

This expression refers to doing something on a limited amount of money.

Origin

"Whatever led to it, the specific association of shoestring with lack of funds has been around since the early 1890s, when references to shoestring gamblers, those who gambled for very small stakes, were first recorded…and the expression has had staying power. However, these days, on a shoestring and shoestring as an adjective can also be somewhat playful and casual."

"Shoestring." Random House. Web, 2 September, 2010 <http://www.randomhouse.com/wotd/index.pperl?date=20010504>.

Web sites used in the chapter

http://bit.ly/dnn5vI	(Center for Disease Control) "Medical Cost Of Obesity."
http://bit.ly/djF62H	(US Dept of Health and Family Services) Calories burned for various activities.
http://nyti.ms/dgicwO	(NY Times) "How To Tame An Inflated Entertainment Budget."
http://bit.ly/ast6T4	(HotDateIdeas.com) Dates on the cheap!
http://bit.ly/9a77YV	(YourSocialWorker.com) Parent-child relationships.
http://bit.ly/cgxrIS	(suite101.com) The importance of family meals.
http://bit.ly/9i4nAz	(PlanetRadioCity.com) Rock star extravagances.
http://bit.ly/a0fx1n	(Get Rich Slowly) "Six Tips For Money Making Hobbies."
http://bit.ly/9aqyFQ	(RandomHouse.com) Definition of the term "shoestring."

Additional resources

Leisure time

http://bit.ly/c8T9TJ	(Move 4 Life) "101 Low-cost Ideas For Worksite Wellness."
http://bit.ly/aJ447v	(About.com) "Best Budget Exercise Equipment."
http://bit.ly/9Kl1QN	(MedicineNet.com) "Burn Calories While You Clean."

Entertain me(nt)

http://bit.ly/9SsSOp	(ZenHabits.net) 100 fun free or cheap activities for kids.
http://bit.ly/cmObj7	(ArtsAlive.ca) Music games, compose your own music.
http://bit.ly/bS9aa2	(BillNye.com) Home-based scientific experiments for kids.

We asked, "How do you keep costs down for activities?" and you said…

We use coupons, take our own food, and buy 2-for-1 deals/season passes. Sometimes if you're going to go somewhere more than one time, buying a season's pass is the better deal because after the second or third visit it's free. We've done that with the zoo.

— **Jennifer Ginn**

We picnic on the living room floor.

— **Elaine Hamill**

By deciding in advance just how much I would spend and then sticking with it.

— **Anonymous**

Movie day—we had a total slug day. No answering phones, no outside world, just the two of us watching movies and creating a makeshift dinner together.

— **Cathy Johnston**

We went on a winter picnic to [the] park. We took hot stew in a thermos and biscuits and watched the waves crash on the shore and we talked.

— **George Reaman**

A nice home cooked meal and a walk on the beach or in the woods. We have never thought that we needed expensive date nights and that was because we could never afford them when we had younger children. So we always loved to walk together and still do.

— **Gord Goral**

Good "spend-no-money" date nights: window shopping at a couple of thrift stores—go for a walk—"rent" movies from the library and make popcorn.

— **Elissa Fenton**

We travelled off season and took food from home. We went camping.

— **Pat Lipop**

Just take day trips from home. Look for events in your area and plan a week or two around them, or take one day to do something bigger like a family boat trip…it is very interesting at the height of the summer as all the watercraft is on the water, water skiers, etc. and nice to see the lovely cottages on the way. A full and exhausting day out, the kids will be asleep before you get home. [An outing to a nearby historical site] is really interesting and a chance to teach a bit of history.

— **Rob Cain**

Many places are negotiable for groups/families but you just have to have enough nerve to ask for a discount. We drive instead of fly. We bring our own food instead of eating out. We camp instead of using a hotel. We try to look for educational, fun and free activities that are provided already—museums, conservation areas, parks, parades, splash pads, etc.

— **David LaFrance**

I always look at bulletin boards at the university, library and other public spaces. Free, or nearly free, activities are always around. We once ended up painting Ukrainian Easter eggs for $5.00, all supplies including eggs provided! [There are] free pottery classes and demonstrations! [There are] *pay what you can* concerts, movies and more.

We always try to attend the community events like farmers markets, festivals, etc. to enjoy all the free, often world-class, entertainment. If all else fails, show up to a performance at the last minute and get ½ price tickets they're selling to attempt to fill the house. Most theaters will show how many seats are left for a performance (not a movie) ahead of time. Check for student/youth/senior/family and other discounts that you may qualify for! We've snagged $250 worth of theater tickets for $40, and still had amazing seats for top notch theater.

— **K. Clarke**

We installed a pool in the backyard.

— **Kim Lauzon**

Leave the kids at home! :)

— **Anonymous**

P.S. A few comments "by the people."

Chapter 9
Money Makes The World Go 'Round
TRAVEL ON LESS

"There's nothing like getting away from it all."

We all know that "money makes the world go 'round" and "it's a small world after all." Since "the world is at your doorstep," let's look at how you can get *more* for *less* when you travel.

Travel today is fast and cheap. You can grab a flight, take a boat, board a train, hop on a bus or jump in your car. Our world has become smaller as the way we get around has changed...and the options for planning and booking your travel have also changed. No longer do we have to make a visit to the travel agency and have the agent take care of everything for us. The Internet has allowed us to become our own travel agent.

Do it yourself or travel agency?

Bill: So, is it always better to book our own travel?

Author: Just because we can do it ourselves, doesn't mean that we should. There are still good reasons to use a travel agent.

A travel agent is a trained professional. She knows the travel business inside and out and can guide you every step of the way. Using an agent to work for you will save you time. You can schedule your appointment, go in to talk about your plans and then leave the arrangements in capable hands. Your agent will help you to make informed decisions and will think of things you may not have. She knows about the sales, deals and discounts that are available. Also, she is obligated to tell you about any extra charges that may be payable so there won't be any surprises.

Make sure that you use an agent from a travel agency that is a member of a traveler advocate organization such as ASTA in the United States and ACTA in Canada. Then if any problems arise, the agent will be there to work on your behalf!!

In any case, you can purchase third party insurance to protect yourself in case the airline or cruise line goes bankrupt.

Factor This In

Benefits of using a travel agent

Save money!—Strong working relationships with travel suppliers and the latest in computer reservations technology enable travel agents to access the most up-to-date information on how to get you the best value.

Traveler advocates—ASTA (The American Society of Travel Agents) has a long-standing record of fighting for consumer rights and ASTA member travel agents are required to adhere to a strict Code of Ethics.

Convenience—The ASTA membership includes travel agents across the country and throughout the world, most of which offer one-stop shopping for all travel arrangements.

Service—ASTA member travel agents are knowledgeable and active in the industry....

Agents will go the extra mile. Agents work for you and will do everything they can to meet your travel needs.

"Why Use A Travel Agent." Travel Sense. Web, 9 July 2010 <http://www.travelsense.org/index.cfm>.

If you are convinced that you can do a better job and do it for less, you can enjoy the benefits of booking your trip online. The main benefits of this method are convenience and the ability to comparison shop. Some of the most popular and well-known sites for the do-it-yourselfer are: Expedia, Travelocity, Orbitz, Priceline or Last Minute Club.

What are the risks of online booking? "A common risk is misrepresentation by online travel agencies, hotels and tour companies. Through the use of special photo techniques, a small beach can be made to look quite a bit larger than it is. The size of a pool, room accommodations and hotel amenities also are misrepresented." (Edmonds, Sydney. "Online Booking: Pros & Cons." eHow. Web, 9 July 2010 <http://www.ehow.com/about_4568828_online-booking-pros-cons.html>.)

Another risk is that an online booking agent may use a "bait and switch" tactic. "Bait and switch is a form of fraud in which the party putting forth the fraud lures in customers by advertising a product or service at a low price or with many features, then reveals to potential customers that the advertised good is not available at the original price or list of assumed features, but something different is.

The goal of the bait and switch is to persuade buyers to purchase the substitute goods as a means of avoiding disappointment over not getting the bait, or as a way to recover sunk costs expended to try to obtain the bait. It suggests that the seller will not show the original product or products advertised but instead will demonstrate a more expensive product or a similar product with a higher margin." ("Bait-and-switch." Wikipedia, The Free Encyclopedia. Wikimedia Foundation, Inc. 30 June 2010. Web, 9 July 2010 <http://en.wikipedia.org/wiki/Bait-and-switch>.)

The unsuspecting buyer is lured in with an unbelievable deal but once the process begins the great price is no longer available.

There is also the danger that the price that was charged to the customer during the online booking was lower than what was actually being charged by the airline or hotel at the time. Because staff can't keep up with the price changes (they may be dealing with thousands of companies) they may still be showing the sale price after the sale ends. It is unlikely that the customer will be compensated. In fact, in order to keep the original booking, the client must pay the price difference.

Bank On It

What to take with you on the trip and what to leave behind

Valuables—leave at home:

• valuable or expensive-looking jewelry

• irreplaceable family objects

• all unnecessary credit cards

• Social Security card, library card, and similar items that may be in your wallet

Do bring medical necessities.

Leave copies of documents and itinerary with relatives [at home] in case they need to contact you in an emergency.

Make two photocopies of the passport identification page, airline tickets, driver's license and the credit cards you plan to take. Leave one copy of each with family or friends at home, and pack the other copies separately from the originals. Leave a copy of the serial numbers of your travelers' checks with a friend or relative at home. Carry your copy with you in a separate place and, as you cash the checks, cross them off the list.

Plan for the unexpected.

Take with you items that you will need if your trip is unexpectedly extended. These items may include extra money or medications.

"Tips For Traveling Abroad." Travel State. U.S. Department of State. Web, July 9 2010 <http://travel.state.gov/travel/tips/tips_1232.html#take_with>.

There is another possible problem with online booking: "One of the most frustrating problems customers of online booking agencies face is that of lost or incorrect records. The customer may receive a confirmation email and their credit card may be charged by the booking agency, but they may later discover that the airline, hotel, or tour company itself has no record of a booking ever being made. In this case, the airline or hotel has no responsibility because the booking was made through a third party." (Kirschbaum, Marie. "Booking online can be risky." Happy News. 2009. Happy Living Magazine. Web, 9 July 2010 <http://www.happynews.com/living/money/consumer-rights-dealing.htm>.)

Don't despair if this happens—contact the agency (within 24 hours) to request a refund. In most cases this will not be a problem. You paid for a booking which was never made. A credit card statement will provide documentation that the money was paid out and will make the refund process easier.

It is important that you understand the risks involved and decide if the lure of lower prices is worth the problems you may have to deal with. We aren't telling you what to do. Many people book their own trips and never have a problem. If this is something you are tempted to do but are worried about it, we have a couple of suggestions for you that offer the benefits and reduce the risks.

When my husband and I were planning to go on a cruise, we knew that there was a good chance that we could find a better price online than what a travel agency might offer us. However, we'd heard a few horror stories and weren't comfortable with booking it ourselves. Someone had mentioned that they went online to research prices for the trip they wanted to take and then brought the information to their travel agent to see if she could match it. It sounded like a good idea to us. We checked out cruise and airline flight prices, printed the information off and took it with us when we visited the travel agency. We were able to get the price matched, have the booking done for us by the agent and feel confident that we had the protection of using an agency.

What if you could use an *online* travel agent to book your trip? "TripAtlas.com, the World's Largest Travel Resource, brings consumers and travel agents together to book holidays online in an easy, simple, and efficient way. Interested travelers visit TripAtlas. com to use the Trip Builder." ("Trip Builder." Trip Atlas. Web, 7 August 2010 <http://tripatlas.com/tripbuilder.html>.)

The Trip Builder asks for your name, contact information, destination, the number of days you plan to stay, and your budget. Your trip request is sent to a global network of professional travel agents (TripAtlas PROs). Agents who specialize in what you are looking for will contact you directly with a price quote on your trip. With a handful of competitive prices in hand, you choose the best deal—and you're set.

You could also consider these websites: Zicasso.com, TravelSense.org and Tripology.com for similar benefits.

Congratulations...you're a winner!

Have you ever been in a store or restaurant and filled out an entry form for a contest and then received a phone call to notify you that you had won? Or you might have been phoned and asked to complete a short survey and told that your name would be entered in a draw for a free trip. Surprise, surprise…a few days later you were notified that you had won. Are you just lucky? No, not really. Everyone else that filled out the form or answered the survey also *won*. (Offers may also come by mail, Internet or fax.)

Avoiding travel scams

Good travel deals are always tempting. After all, paying less for a vacation can mean more money for touring, souvenirs, or for another vacation. Even though there are some great legitimate travel deals out there, it always pays to be on the lookout for scams. Here are a few precautions you should take:

- **Work with a recognized travel agency.** One way to minimize your travel risk is to work with a recognized travel agency and travel counselor.

- **Purchase trip cancellation insurance.** If purchasing trip cancellation insurance—look for the type that covers the suppliers going out of business and not just the insurance that provides coverage in the event of sickness, etc.

- **Pay with a credit card.** Credit cards are the safest way to pay for purchases because you can dispute the charges if you don't get the services you were promised or the offer was misrepresented. Most credit card issuers will remove the charges completely if you report the problem promptly.

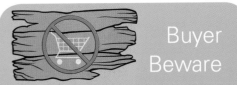

Buyer Beware

Shopping on the Internet

If you purchase travel services online be sure you have the following information about the Internet seller:

- the business name, address and telephone number

- a clear description of exactly what you are purchasing

- a clear description of any additional charges that may apply to the contract

- the currency in which the amount owing is payable

- the terms, conditions and method of payment

- the supplier's cancellation, return, exchange and refund policies, if any

- confirmation that you will receive a copy of the contract in writing, or in electronic form, including the delivery date (the contract should include the information disclosed to you, as well as your name and the date the contract was entered into)

Before giving your credit card number or other financial information to a business, make sure that the merchant has a secure transaction system. Most Internet browsers indicate when you are using a secure Internet link. Check for:

- a website address that starts with https://, or

- an icon, often a lock or an unbroken key, at the bottom of the screen

"Avoiding Travel Scams." Justice and Attorney General. Government of Saskatchewan. Web, 9 July 2010 <http://www.justice.gov.sk.ca/travel>.

Bank On It

Travel offers

"If it sounds too good to be true, it probably is." Read the fine print on all travel offers, especially those offering free vacation packages!

Travel services usually have to be paid for before they are delivered, which creates opportunities for disreputable individuals or companies. Consumers who receive offers by phone or mail for a free or extremely low-priced vacation trip should be cautious. Consumers should instead ask for written information to be sent to them....Consumers should not make immediate decisions before researching.

If a consumer is told he or she has been given a free vacation, they should ask if a purchase is required. Some packages have promoted free air fare, as long as the consumer pays for expensive hotel arrangements. Consumers should also obtain a confirmed departure date, in writing, before they pay anything and be skeptical of promises that an acceptable date will be arranged later. If the destination is a beach resort, consumers should check with both the seller and the hotel on the distance between the beach and the hotel.

Consumers who decide to go forward with the trip after checking out the details should use credit, since this option gives consumers legal rights to pursue a chargeback if the promised services are not delivered.

"Travel Offers." NYS Consumer. Consumer Protection Board. Web, 9 July 2010 <http://www.nysconsumer.gov/clahm/airlines.htm#travel_offers>.

- **Avoid high pressure sales.** Don't be pressured into "limited time" offers. If you are pressured to make an immediate decision because there are only "a few of these bargain deals left," just say no.

- **Be aware of restrictions.** Often the best travel deals are only available for off-peak times, not during school vacations, holidays or other popular travel dates.

- **Read the contract.** Never sign a contract before you read and understand it. If the salesperson promises you something that is not in the contract, DO NOT SIGN IT unless those promises are added officially. If it is not in the contract it does not exist.

- **Confirm the arrangements.** If transportation and hotel are included in the travel package, ask how to contact those companies and confirm with them directly that the reservations have been made.

- **Know exactly what's included.** A "free" or incredibly cheap trip may have hidden costs.

- **Confirm the departure date.** Get a confirmed departure date, in writing, before you pay anything.

- **Do your own travel research.** It's easy to get information from a local travel agent and other sources such as newspapers, books, and the Internet. You may be able to get the trip you want for far less than the "bargain" price a company is offering.

- **Be skeptical of offers for "free" trips.** Airlines and other well-known companies sometimes operate contests for travel prizes. However, there are also companies that offer "free" trips to try to lure people into buying their products or services. It's never "free" if you have to pay something.

- **Be cautious about unsolicited emails for travel.** They are often fraudulent. ("Avoiding Travel Scams." Justice and Attorney General. Government of Saskatchewan. Web, 9 July 2010 <http://www.justice.gov.sk.ca/travel>.)

If you get taken in a scam, there may be some recourse available. You can contact local consumer advocates by phone, mail or email. Check out the additional resources for contact information.

Save a buck

Reward miles

So you want to use reward miles for travel? Some times are better than others for using your air miles—in other words, the benefit will be greater. Keep these tips in mind before you cash in your air miles:

- Take into consideration the cost of each flight—perhaps you will want to use your air miles for the most expensive flights.

- If you are planning to travel during peak seasons the price of airfare will be higher. Plan in advance and use your reward points.

- Traveling with the family is expensive, reward miles will help to keep the cost of the vacation down and free up money to use when you arrive at your destination. Book early.

- Don't let your miles expire—plan trips before that happens.

- Check for opportunities to use discounted versions of the award ticket.

How else can you use those frequent flyer rewards? Sure, you can use them to fly but you can also use them to get upgrades on your seats. You may be able to swap miles for hotel loyalty points and awards and use them for free accommodations or room upgrades. Points can be used for car rental vouchers for discounts and free rental days. Rewards can also be redeemed for vouchers for products. Finally, if points are about to expire or you just don't want to use them, you can gift them to family and friends or to a charitable organization.

Coupons—not just for groceries

Remember we talked about using coupons when you grocery shop? How about using them when you travel? According to Stephanie Nelson, *The Coupon Mom*, if you are looking for online coupons for air fares you can go to SideStep.com or Travelocity.com. SideStep also has a "compare hotels" tool for cheaper accommodations, and if you are looking for airport parking, you can check LongTermParking.com for coupons for many of the airport parking lots. Once you are settled and looking for something to do, you can use the coupons you printed off these websites: Entertainment.com for car rentals, hotel rates, dining and attractions, and for dining: Valpak.com, HotCoupons.com or Restaurant.com.

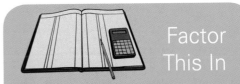

Factor This In

Tips when choosing reward cards

These are points to consider when choosing a credit card reward program:

- Some airlines only allow a limited number of seats that can be "purchased" with air miles. Choose a reward program that protects you against this possibility.

- Find out if there are levels (of spending) that must be reached before higher rewards are earned.

- How much do the reward points cost you? Before you earn "x" amount of rewards, how much do you have to spend?

- Does the reward program match your spending habits?

- If there is an annual fee, is it worth it?

- Do the reward points max out after a certain level of spending?

You may find free packages (with coupons for local attractions, restaurants and stores) at visitor's bureaus and on their websites for the locations you plan to visit. Nelson offers more help on her website, TheCouponMom.com, to find and use online coupons.

Bed and breakfast

A touch of home away from home, a bed and breakfast usually offers a room with a bathroom, for overnight lodging and a breakfast in the morning. These establishments are most often in a private home and are staffed by the home owners and have less than ten bedrooms available. It is a more intimate setting and can cost less than a traditional hotel room.

House swaps

When you travel your house sits empty and unused. You have to pay for accommodations when you travel and there's no break on your house expenses while you are away—the mortgage and taxes still have to be paid, the utility companies still want their share as well. While you are in France, a French family is in the same situation paying their home expenses while also paying for a place to stay in the United States. It seems a shame to have two empty houses, doesn't it?

If you can relate to this scenario and you find it frustrating, you might consider arranging a house swap when you plan your vacation. There are exchange groups online (there may or may not be a membership fee) where you can register your home information, browse the listings, contact other members and when you find a match, sign a contract.

Here are three different types of home exchanges:

- "In a *traditional exchange*, you and your exchange partner travel at the same time and stay in each other's primary residences."

- "In *non-simultaneous exchanges*...exchange partners come to stay in a vacation home or secondary residence while the owner continues to live in his or her own primary home."

- "A third type of exchange, known as a *hospitality exchange*, involves you and your trading partner taking turns staying as guests in each other's primary homes." (Adapted from: "Home Exchange: How-to Guide." Independent Traveler. Web, 9 July 2010 <http://www.independenttraveler.com/resources/article.cfm?AID=39&category=7>.)

Fool's Gold

Extravagant trips

Paris

You can travel to Paris in a private jet, spend a week in a suite at the Ritz, enjoy private tours and around the clock concierge service, and dine at the finest of restaurants for $300,000.

British Columbia

Looking for a vacation heli-skiing in beautiful British Columbia with a private helicopter at your service? There's room for 8 people and three guides and your spot will cost $21,000. Half of the week is spent in a swanky lodge, and the rest of the week at Halcyon Hot Springs Village and Spa.

Miami

Miami Beach's Hotel Victor will provide a penthouse suite, and in-room treatments from the spa staff for $11,000. You'll also be provided with food and drink—of course in this case you will *bathe* in the drink—a tubful of Evian Natural Spring Water.

Adapted from: Pergament, Danielle. "World's Most Extravagant Trips." Concierge. Web, 9 July 2010 <http://www.concierge.com/ideas/luxury/tours/1726>. For more indulgent possibilities, check out Concierge.com.

Hit the road, Jack!

Let's forget all the planes, trains and boats and opt for a road trip instead. There are many advantages to being able to just jump in the car—there's a lot of flexibility in time and cost. You can go for a day, a weekend, a week—whatever fits into your schedule. You can combine the trip (or plan it around) other events—business trips, family reunions, or weddings, etc.

Before you leave on your trip, you should buy a map, get a map book from your automobile association or purchase software for the GPS. If you are going to make road trips a regular part of your travel plans, you could investigate club memberships that will get you restaurant, hotel and local attraction discounts. (Make sure that you bring the card with you when you travel.)

If there are particular sights you want to visit then plan it out ahead of time. If you are worried about where you will stay overnight then make your reservations ahead of time. When you bring a cooler and pack healthy snacks and water, it will be easier to avoid junk food and will also help to keep food costs down.

Since it is a road trip and you will be depending on your vehicle make sure that the car is "up to speed."

"Here are a few things to check before leaving on a driving holiday:

- Check all your fluid levels before leaving.

- Good spark plugs and a clean air filter add up to better gas mileage.

- Check your tires for wear and alignment.

- Get your brakes checked.

- Check your cooling system. Make certain your radiator isn't clogged, and all the hoses and belts in your engine are working properly.

- Be prepared for trouble. Make certain you have a good spare tire, tire changing tools, an extra bottle of water for your radiator, and a flashlight.

- After a rest stop and at the beginning of each travel day, always walk around your vehicle and check for anything unusual before you resume your trip." ("Summer Driving Tips." British Columbia. Province of British Columbia. Web, 9 July 2010 <http://www.th.gov.bc.ca/popular-topics/driver_info/summer/summer.htm>.)

Do The Math

10 volunteer opportunities for free travel

The chance to give something back, to meet other travelers or simply to meet the locals and an opportunity to share your skills and knowledge:

1. WWOOF (Willing Workers on Organic Farms), worldwide

2. Turtle Teams, worldwide [help threatened sea turtles]

3. Conservation Volunteers, Australia and New Zealand [working in teams to protect habitats and promote eco tourism]

4. Sudan Volunteer Programme, Sudan [teach English]

5. Appalachian Trail Conference, USA [help with trail building and maintenance]

6. Trip Leader for HF Holidays, Europe [lead their walking holidays]

7. Help Exchange, worldwide [worldwide hosts that are looking for an extra pair of hands]

8. Peace Corps, worldwide [live and work in another country]

9. United Nations Volunteers, worldwide [from health care and economic development to assisting after natural disasters]

10. Kibbutz Volunteer, Israel [live as part of a socialist community]

Be sure to thoroughly research any options before undertaking a project.

Adapted from: Scott, Matt. "Ten Volunteer Opportunities For Free Travel." Matador Network. Julie Schwietert Collazo. 2 July 2008. Web, 9 July 2010 <http://matadorchange.com/10-volunteer-opportunities-for-free-travel/>.

Your Money's Worth

Reduce travel costs

- Plan ahead. Are there friends or family members that you can stay with so that you can save money on hotels? If not, you may find booking early saves you money.

- Can you drive instead of flying to your destination? It could be cheaper to drive especially if there are lots of people traveling together. Driving also allows you to bring food along to reduce meal costs.

- Figure out your travel budget and stick to your plan. Think about car rentals, travel and accommodation costs and food costs.

- Look for flight and hotel deals online.

- If you are booking a hotel, try to find one that includes breakfast. When looking for a restaurant, perhaps the hotel personnel can direct you to local restaurants offering good value. Pick up food at local grocery stores for some *make it yourself* meals. (Be cautious about border crossing regulations re: food, if you are traveling to another country.)

- Check out the local sites that are free or low-cost. Do your research online ahead of time and visit tourist centers. Be sure to look for discounts on hotels, restaurants and local attractions.

Getting a second opinion

Before you make your final travel plans why not talk to the experts—your fellow travelers. You can hear what *everyday* people have to say about a particular destination and their personal experiences? Check out these websites:

1. TripAdvisor.com—contains over 35 million traveler reviews and opinions.

2. TravelPost.com—puts together user-reviews to save their readers time, money and trouble when traveling.

3. Hotelicopter.com—lets you post and share hotel reviews with your friends and you can see your friends' reviews.

4. SpottedByLocals.com—it has a series of blogs about local travel—not the tourist stuff.

And here are suggestions for some websites that help you to save on flights and accommodations/attractions once you arrive:

1. Yapta.com—"Track flight prices and save money before and after you buy! Track flight prices BEFORE you buy, Yapta email alerts let you know when prices drop and when to buy to save money on airfare. Get airline refunds AFTER you buy. If the price of your flight drops below what you paid, Yapta helps you get a refund for the difference." ("Track Flight Prices And Save Money Before And After You Buy!" Yapta. Web, 7 August 2010 <http://www.yapta.com/>.)

2. CheapFlights.com—"Find the best travel deals and cheap airline tickets from one of our many partners: Virgin Atlantic, Expedia, Orbitz, jetBlue, PriceLine.com, AA.com, CheapAir.com, British Airways, Cheap Tickets." ("Find Cheap Airline Tickets." Cheap Flights. Web, 7 August 2010 < http://www.cheapflights.com/>.)

3. NotForTourists.com—"Not For Tourists is the ultimate guide for the savvy city-dweller. Our philosophy is simple: Whether you've lived in your neighborhood for 55 years or 55 minutes, NFT will help you navigate and explore the city like a local. Written and designed by in-the-know city slickers themselves, NFT is mobile-oriented, cartographically-inclined, and to-the-point." ("About." Not For Tourists. Web, 7 August 2010 < http://www.notfortourists.com/default.aspx>.)

Off the beaten path

Are you feeling the penny pinch but still want a holiday? Why not vacation at home? Before we ever heard the term *staycation*, my husband and I were using this strategy. We had four children and income was low and costs were high and it was too expensive to have couple time away from home. We couldn't afford to pay for a hotel for a weekend away so we found *lodgings* for our children and we stayed at home instead. We used the time to come and go from our house as we pleased—a novelty with young children—and spent our money on eating out or dining in. We picked up movies and enjoyed treats during our *at home* movie night. It was relaxing, fun and inexpensive.

Penny: This sounds like something that might work for us. Do you have any guidelines to make this staycation *into a real vacation?*

Author: Make sure you treat it like one. Circle the date on your calendar so you have a beginning and an end. Remember that "two's company and three's a crowd." You don't want visitors to drop in unexpectedly so let people know that you won't be available during this time. You don't have to answer the phone or the door. Let me rephrase that last sentence: Don't answer the phone or the door—unless you are expecting a pizza delivery!

Make sure you stick to your budget. You can entertain yourselves with low-cost fun activities. Bring out the games, watch movies, read books, have a spa night and look after each other. This is about having time alone, enjoying each other's company, pampering yourself and your loved one and kicking back and relaxing.

Penny: I think I'll find out when my parents have some free time to take the kids. I feel more relaxed already!!

Makes Cents

Vacation at home

You've decided to stay at home this year for your holidays. Make sure that you take some time to clean the house and get the laundry and shopping done ahead so that you can enjoy a nice, clean home. Plan your activities ahead. If you'll be eating at home then load up on fun, quick-to-prepare food items.

Here's some ideas for turning your *staycation* into a real holiday:

- Kick back at home.
- Have breakfast on the patio.
- Catch up on those little things you can never find time to do (not housework—fun things!)
- Read a book/throw in a movie/ linger in bed/take a nap.
- Stay in your pajamas all day.
- Pamper yourself (or each other).

If you decide to leave the house:

- Go shopping.
- Dine out.
- Go to the movie theater.
- Have a beach day/picnic.
- Tour your home town.
- Go to an amusement park or other local attraction.
- Get a massage.

Think of your own fun ideas...the idea is to save money, relax and have fun!

However you choose to *vacation* you can find creative ways to keep your costs down and still have a great time. When you want to travel but your budget is limited, get creative—after all "creativity is the mother of invention"—and use some of the ideas that we've just shared.

If you are looking for more resources for *cheap and creative* travel advice, Rebecca Waer, writer for the LA Budget Travel Examiner, gives her top 5 travel site choices:

1. NY Times' Frugal Traveler [http://nyti.ms/bo2cNj]

2. MatadorNetwork.com

3. NY Times' Practical Traveler [http://nyti.ms/bksAtd]

4. TravelChannel.com

5. RoadTripUSA.com

(Waer, Rebecca. "Top Five Travel Sites: Creative Travel Ideas For Budgets Big And Small." Examiner. 11 May 2010. Web, 9 July 2010 <http://www.examiner.com/x-7416-LA-Budget-Travel-Examiner~y2009m5d11-Top-5-surefire-websites-for-travel-ideas>.)

And the five best travel sites according to the editors of the Budget Travel website are:

1. Dohop.com

2. Kayak.com

3. PriceLine.com

4. TripAdvisor.com

5. Venere.com

(Tuttle, Brad. "5 Best Travel Sites." Budget Travel. 19 May 2009. Web, 9 July 2010 <http://www.budgettravel.com/bt-dyn/content/article/2009/05/19/AR2009051901143.html>.)

We advise the serious budget traveler to take a few minutes to check these websites out and see what they have to offer. You have nothing to lose and if not *everything*, at least *a lot*, to gain.

We make these suggestions:

- "To be or not to be" your own travel agent, you decide.

- Get the best of both worlds with online agents.

- Don't get scammed on your vacation.

- Reward yourself with lower travel costs.

- Road trip anyone?

- Listen to the travel experts—your fellow travelers!

- Vacation at home.

Common Cents

"When preparing to travel, lay out all your clothes and all your money. Then take half the clothes and twice the money."

- Susan Heller

"Living on Earth may be expensive, but it includes an annual free trip around the Sun."

- Unknown

"After a visit to the beach, it's hard to believe that we live in a material world."

- Pam Shaw

We've looked at using an agent and being your own agent. We've discussed the pros and cons of each method and suggested a middle-of-the-road alternative. We want to make sure that you don't get taken by a scam artist when you make your travel plans. We've looked at ways to reduce your travel costs by using coupons or reward miles or even by "swapping" houses to save on the cost of accommodations. There's a lot to see in your own neck of the woods and road trips are a great alternative. Even day trips can be a lot of fun and they bring the cost of holidaying down—so you can afford to go more often! You can let other people who have gone before you guide you through your trip as they provide reviews on hotels, restaurants and the attractions at your destination of choice. You don't even have to leave your home to have a holiday—just observe a few rules and a *staycation* can be your way to get away from it all. After all, it's true what they say—there's no place like home.

We hope you're not too tired after all that vacation talk because it's time to party...

Web sites used in the chapter

http://bit.ly/9NcERT	(TravelSense.org) "Why Use A Travel Agent?"
http://bit.ly/976ilf	(eHow.com) Pros and cons of booking online.
http://bit.ly/clRS7i	(Wikipedia) A definition of "bait and switch."
http://bit.ly/a1ktu5	(US Dept. of State) "Tips For Traveling Abroad."
http://bit.ly/bcrGRA	(HappyNews.com) Consumer rights dealing with online travel booking agencies.
http://bit.ly/14ww5m	(Trip Atlas) Online travel agents.
http://bit.ly/bjih2p	(Gov. of Saskatchewan) "Travel Frauds, Scams, And Consumer Alerts."
http://bit.ly/croSZa	(NYSConsumer.gov) "Travel Offers."
http://bit.ly/ZemJx	(CouponMom.com) "Coupons, Grocery Coupons And Online Coupons."
http://bit.ly/bFAckS	(IndependentTraveler.com) "Home Exchange: How-to Guide."
http://bit.ly/amxBYX	(Concierge.com) "World's Most Extravagant Trips."
http://bit.ly/9YpRbe	(British Columbia Ministry of Transportation) Summer travel checklist.
http://bit.ly/bFfdji	(MatadorChange.com) "10 Volunteer Opportunities For Free Travel."
http://bit.ly/CDep	(Yapta.com) Track flight prices.
http://bit.ly/rCSWO	(CheapFlights.com) Best travel deals.
http://bit.ly/lFWux	(NotForTourists.com) Explore any city like a local.
http://bit.ly/bHWCJ7	(Examiner.com) "Top Five Travel Sites: Creative Travel Ideas For Budgets Big And Small."
http://bit.ly/bLoXIq	(BudgetTravel.com) "5 Best Travel Sites."
http://bit.ly/15pt4h	(CNN Money) "Who Gets The Most Vacation?"

Additional resources

Do it yourself or travel agency?

http://bit.ly/9Crje3	(PriceLine.com) Shop for discount travel.
http://bit.ly/beHtH9	(Expedia.com) Plan your trip and find great deals.
http://bit.ly/bLGoYU	(Travelocity.ca) Plan your trip and find great deals.

Congratulations… you're a winner!

http://bit.ly/9HVtQ7	(Federal Trade Commission) Reporting travel fraud.
http://bit.ly/asi2Ny	(ConsumerFraudReporting.org) Check for latest travel frauds and scams.
http://bit.ly/b05uiG	(MSNBC) "Top 5 Travel Scams."

Save a buck

http://bit.ly/cMUYsJ	(eHow.com) Tips for using flyer miles.
http://bit.ly/9qu70m	(BedAndBreakfast.com) Bed and breakfast directory.
http://bit.ly/8XMUSW	(HomeExchange.com) Home exchange network.

Hit the road, Jack!

http://bit.ly/a6wQNp	(RoadTripAmerica.com) Routes planning for road trips.
http://bit.ly/dfDsqM	(eHow.com) "How To Take A Road Trip On A Budget."
http://bit.ly/9Nb9Hu	(GasBuddy.com) Find the cheapest gas pump near you.

Getting a second opinion

http://bit.ly/9ML9qy	(MyTravelAgents.com) Find a local travel agent.
http://bit.ly/98iEnp	(TravelPost.com) Hotel reviews and information.
http://bit.ly/aWXjFt	(Debbies Caribbean Resort Reviews) Find a travel agent.

Off the beaten path

http://bit.ly/ddB8NO	(USA)(StaycationDirectory.com) Vacation locally.
http://bit.ly/bh5IcP	(About.com) "Top 10 Staycation Strategies."
http://bit.ly/b3o5rJ	(NotForTourists.com) Local maps and reviews.

We asked, "How do you cut down your costs on vacations?" and you said...

We have visited tourist information booths and received coupons for money off on admission to attractions. We take our own lunches and picnic rather than buy meals. We take day trips to attractions close to home to save on accommodation costs. We go to some places in the off season; it is usually cheaper then. We check online for special deals at places we would like to visit.

— **Teri Reaman**

Don't eat out a lot. Prepare meals where you are staying or find places with good continental breakfasts.

— **Joanne Charlesworth**

I usually pack snacks and games, etc. to keep the kids busy and full. Buying all your meals on the road can be very expensive. I also try to purchase things at grocery stores where possible to keep meal costs down like cheese/crackers, and cold drinks.

— **Gail Hoskin**

Ask for better prices. For vacations, often travelling at a different time for the same vacation will be cheaper. Utilize PriceLine. com and HotWire.com where hotels would be required.

— **Doug Elliot**

On a recent trip driving through the USA we discovered that we could save a lot of money by not booking ahead for motels. We found coupon books at the various road side rest stop areas for hotels, restaurants, and other places of interest to tourists and travelers. By taking our time to see the sights we wanted to see and travel at a comfortable pace, we would wait until we were ready to stop for the day and would call local motels listed in the coupon book. We stayed in reputable motel chains that we were familiar with, often for $20 - $30 per night including breakfast in the morning.

— **Jim MacDonald**

Our family just loves a hotel room with a pool!!! Using the online travel sites where you can set your own price helps us keep the costs within our budget—you have to be a bit flexible with your dates—staying away from the weekends and hot spots—but even those small cities and towns have cool places to see and discover and who doesn't love the little bottles of shampoo!!! Use the kitchen and microwave in the room for breakfast and lunches and you can keep it cheap. We also look for restaurants that offer "kids eat for free" nights!

— **Gavin Bourne**

Packing food and sleeping in the van when possible.

— **Kathy Bruno**

We visit friends we have made over the Internet, sharing their accommodations when we visit them, and hosting them when they visit us, rather than going to hotels.

— **George Harris**

We have taken trips to our backyard!! (Kids don't make it easy to get out.) Our date night calendar consists of things like sharing a milkshake under the stars, a candlelit bath and other fun "trips." We also went on a cruise for our 10th anniversary and watched a horrible time share presentation for a free trip.

— **Amanda Renaud**

We don't take many vacations but when we do we usually stay with friends.

— **Max Barter**

Watch for seat sales and go all inclusive.

— **Marion Penney**

Bring our own food and drinks for a day outing. While staying in a hotel pay the extra and upgrade to a kitchenette. That way you are able to eat breakfast in your room and bring food on your outings. You really do end up ahead.

— **Anonymous**

We try to travel in a non-peak season, pack picnics, use coupons and discount flyers. We learned many theme parks also charge lower rates if we go later in the day and then we also avoid the larger early morning crowds.

— **Heather McAlpine**

Plan ahead and search out for deals. Buy all inclusive or stay at a place with a kitchen to prepare meals. Research ahead for rental items and things you can take yourself.

— **Susan Richards**

When I book a cruise with my agent I pay $x. If the price goes down I get the new lower price. If the price goes up I stay at the price I booked it at. Waiting until the last minute doesn't get you a better deal anymore. It gets you the rooms no one else wanted—like a suite at full fare.

— **Jackie Brooks**

P.S. A few comments "by the people."

Chapter 10

Have Your Cake And Eat It Too

HOW TO PARTY CHEAP

"Happy birthday, Honey!"

Contrary to what you may believe, we do agree with *Kool and the Gang*; we think that you should "celebrate good times"—babies, birthdays, weddings, graduations and anniversaries. We aren't party poopers…who doesn't like a good party? We just think that you can have a great time and stay on budget.

We will divide this chapter into two sections: party planning and gift giving. We'll look at ways to put together a party and keep the costs from spiraling out of control. Then we'll (briefly) look at ways to reduce your costs when buying gifts.

We're having a party

When it's time to put on a party, you need to think about the why, what, where, who and how. Each of these factors will impact the overall cost of the event.

Why are you having a party? Are you celebrating a birthday or an anniversary? Is it a graduation party or a religious celebration? You may be celebrating an engagement or the birth of a child. Is it a housewarming, farewell party or a family reunion? Are you celebrating a holiday or do you just want to have fun? No matter what reason you can think of, you can have a party for it.

What will you do at the party? Is it a pool party, a barbeque, a games night, a pajama party or a costume party? Is it a dinner party, dance party, formal party, casual party, or a beach party?

Where will you hold your party, in your home or in the backyard? Will you go to the beach or the local park or will you need to rent a hall? Maybe you and your guests can meet somewhere for an activity—no cooking and clean up necessary.

Who will be invited to your party? Once you know the why, what and where of your party, you'll know who and how many people you can invite. Make your guest list based on the room available, your budget, the type of party you're planning, and then consider how well your guests will get along with each other and whether they will be willing to participate in the activities you have planned. You do want to have fun after all and you want your guests to be comfortable and to have an enjoyable time.

How will you let people know about your party? Are you making phone calls, sending emails or mailing invitations? Is it word-of-mouth, bring a buddy or by formal invitation only?

Keep it down (the cost that is)

Location

Probably the cheapest place to hold a party is in your own home. There are some potential problems, however. Your home may be too small or not set up to make a party enjoyable. That's what friends and family are all about!! Does anyone have a home large enough to host the party, and would be willing to let you use it?

Can you move your party outside into the backyard? Space is less of an issue in that case. You can set up a canopy to provide shelter from the sun or rain. If your backyard doesn't work, is there a park that you can use? Perhaps you can find an outdoor location that has other facilities you can make use of. We've had get-togethers at a beach that also had a wading pool, playground equipment, swimming pool and mini golf course.

Churches and other organizations often offer their facilities or meeting rooms for free to church members. If not, there may be a reduced fee. In any case, this option can be an economical choice even if you don't attend the church. Check out local community centers—you do need to check around because the price can vary greatly. A local bed & breakfast may be willing to host your party. Out of town guests can stay there and if you give them enough business you may get free use of their property and facilities.

Arrange to meet at a restaurant and book one of their dining spaces. You can head to the bowling alley or other amusement center for your party. You will have to pay for the meal/activity but the room is provided. And you don't have to clean up!!

Invitations

Getting the word out about your celebration can be both expensive and time consuming—and since *time is money* we've put together a list of resources that will help you keep costs down and spare your precious time.

If you are going for a more traditional feel with your invitations, you can visit VistaPrint.com for "custom printed invitations and announcements." You have a choice of these events: birthday, general party, wedding, baby, business, moving, religious or holiday.

Makes Cents

Save on your next party

1. **Prioritize.** Spend your budget on the most important things.

2. **Invite with care.** More people = higher costs.

3. **Get creative.** Make your own invitations, email or hand deliver them.

4. **Simplify.** Decorations, party supplies and the menu can be simplified.

5. **Shop online.** Look at the large party stores and comparison shop. Look for discounts and coupons.

6. **Plan ahead.** If you buy in bulk the prices will usually be lower and you will have supplies for the next party.

7. **Shop around.** Look for clearance items and shop off season when planning for holiday celebrations and special events.

Right On The Money

How much does an (average) wedding cost?

It's easy to see why $29,000 is the average wedding cost. Consider the [following] example....It falls short of the average $29,000 wedding cost, but you'll see how it adds up.

- church/officiant Fee: $500

- reception site rental: $2,500

- food: $40/plate x 100 = $4,000

- photographer: $2,000

- DJ or band: $1,500

- flowers: $750

- cake: $500

- rings: $5,000

- dress/tux: $500

- open bar: $3,500

- total: $20,750

Obviously, this example isn't for a cheap wedding, but for 100 people, it's probably a modest one. Any of the above costs can vary greatly based upon your choices, and could easily skyrocket.

Adapted from: Weliver, David. "How Much Does An (Average) Wedding Cost?" Money Under 30. 2 June 2009. Web, 10 July 2010 <http://www.moneyunder30.com/how-much-average-wedding-cost>.

When you use VistaPrint.com, you can choose from their designs, hire a design specialist or use a design of your own creation. You can even upload your own photos. Choose your design (matching envelopes, if you like), the size, add your info and submit it—all online from the comfort of your computer chair. (There is also a section with free products on the website.)

If you are ready for the virtual world, you can find free resources to fill your need. Microsoft Office Online has a wide choice of party invitation templates that you can use. You can download, edit and print the invitations or flyers or email them as an e-card. You can share them with your friends, family members and colleagues on social bookmarking sites (like Del.icio.us, Digg, Facebook, Live Favorites, etc.).

Here's another resource: "Smilebox can help you kick off your bash with dazzling invitations. Whatever the occasion, these invites will definitely grab their attention.

Just choose the design you like and add the party details…Don't forget to look for matching thank you cards to follow up on the fun!

Print your invitations out at home or at a local store. You can also quickly email your invites and your guests can RSVP right in the comments section. How cool is that?" ("Celebrate With Fun Party Invitations!" Smilebox. Web, 10 July 2010 <http://www.smilebox.com/invitations/>.)

MyInvitationLink.com is a website that will "host" your invitations for a fee, based on the length of time you choose—three months, six months or one year. There's no limit to the number of people you send out the invitations to and you can change the pictures, templates and music. It also includes RSVP management.

Obviously, if you choose the traditional route, your guests will return an RSVP card which you will include in the invitation envelope, or you can ask them to respond by phone or by email. With an e-card sent from your own email address, the guest will respond back to the same address. (If you go this route you may consider setting up a separate email just for this purpose to make it easier to track.) Electronic RSVPs save both postage and time since the response is free and instantaneous.

If you are looking for convenience for your guests and ease of tracking for yourself you might consider making use of one of the online services available. Here are a few sites that provide these RSVP services: Evite.com, MyPunchBowl.com, RsvpHQ.com, Sendomatic.com and Zoji.com.

There are also "do it yourself event websites" at MyEvent.com—standard and premium packages, with monthly or yearly rates. They offer a free seven day trial to try it out before you commit to using their service.

Why not create a website? "Instead of phoning your list of guests, simply send an email pointing them to your website to read up on all the event information. All the details and maps are accessible at all times (and from anywhere). Guests will have one place to find all the answers to their questions regarding where and when the events take place, and how to get there." ("Why An Event Website." My Event. Web, 10 July 2010 <http://www.party.myevent.com/1/why_a_website.htm>.)

Facebook.com is also a popular free platform for creating event web pages including invitations and RSVPs.

When you want to send invitions and stay organized, these are just a few of the many websites available to help you with your party planning.

Decorations and supplies

If you want to save money on decorations and party supplies, preplan for your party by purchasing your decorations during store *after sales*, buying supplies in bulk and sharing with friends, asking friends and family to contribute from their stash, or by sponsoring a contest (to gather decorations, party favors and/or game ideas—most creative contributor wins).

When possible, keep the decorations, store them and then reuse them on another occasion. Make your own decorations or enlist a friend to help.

You can create or purchase edible centerpieces which do double duty—they serve as both a beautiful decoration and a delicious part of your menu.

Buyer Beware

The top 10 gifts you shouldn't buy your wife this Christmas

10. **Tools.** Unless she's a handywoman…

9. **A vacuum.** Any cleaning or kitchen appliance says, "Honey, clean the house for me."

8. **A cookbook.** She wants to be reminded how she is special and appreciated…not given more work to do.

7. **Clothes.** You must keep in mind that women are shaped very differently and sizes can vary…

6. **Tickets to the monster truck rally.** [No explanation needed.]

5. **Tires.** [Unless they come with a new car.]

4. **Computer equipment.** This isn't the time to buy hardware or software…

3. **Socks.** [Duh!]

2. **Fruitcake.** [Ugh!]

1. **Membership to a diet program.** [No comment necessary.]

Wang, Laurie. "The Top 10 Gifts You Shouldn't Buy Your Wife This Christmas." Power To Change. Web, 10 July 2010 <http://powertochange.com/culture/christmasgifts/>.

[We believe this list is applicable ANY time—not just at Christmas.]

Discount stores have lots of items to choose from for your party decorations and supplies. Many of these stores have a section dedicated to party supplies. Look for tableware, balloons, party favors, streamers, and banners. (Don't forget the safety tips we gave you in chapter 5 about shopping at discount stores.)

Party supply stores or warehouses, like Party Packagers, Party America, Party Land and Party Maker (notice a theme?), offer the convenience of being able to pick up supplies and go—no shipping charges or waiting for items to arrive and hoping they get there on time. There is a physical location so you can visit and see what's available, and get ideas for your party. They are probably less expensive than shopping at a department store and most likely more expensive than the discount store. These specialty stores offer convenience and selection. You can also rent machines—snow cone, popcorn, cotton candy, slushy machines, but also things like tables and chairs. The big chains also have e-stores.

Speaking of e-stores, if you want to shop around for better prices, but don't want to drive from store to store, you can go to the Internet to do your shopping. Besides party supplies (like dinnerware and tablecloths), party favors and decorations (banners, balloons, streamers, etc.), online party supplies stores offer party themes, planning lists, games and party projects. They are the *go-to* for *how-to* party. The sites often have promotions, discounts, clubs and coupons for you to take advantage of as well. They may also offer party planning, decorating services and rentals. You'll have to factor in costs and time when ordering online as you may have to pay for shipping and you will have to wait for your items to be delivered.

You can also check out websites like: iParty.com, Shindigz.com, ThemePartyMall.com, PartyThemeShop.com or PartyBasic.com (don't forget the stores we mentioned in the second paragraph—PartyPackagers.com, PartyAmerica.com, PartyLand.com and PartyMakerDiscountMegastore.com) to see some of what's available online.

Just a reminder that you shouldn't forget about your circle of family members, friends and co-workers that may have equipment, supplies, talents, skills and other resources available for you to draw on when you are planning your party. They may be willing to share what they have when you need it. While we believe you should take advantage of these resources, we suggest that you don't take *advantage* of their generosity. Also, if you do get help from them, you should be willing to reciprocate in kind when they are looking for help. If you're not willing to give back, then don't ask in the first place!

Food

Buying, cooking and preparing the food from scratch are the most economical ways to put together the refreshments for your party. However, it can also be labor-intensive and time consuming.

Don't have the time, energy or inclination to make the food yourself? Or if the party is just too large to manage on your own then why not have the meal catered? Many church groups are looking for ways to raise money and if church women can't cook, who can? The women's group at my mother's church prepared and served a roast beef dinner for my wedding reception that was delicious and extremely cost-efficient.

Another idea is to buy pre-made food, then put it out buffet style and have your guests help themselves or hire someone to serve it for you and do the clean up too. There may be a local youth group looking to raise some money that would be willing to do the work.

Bill: I'd like to have friends over more often but even though I help out, Penny feels that it's pretty overwhelming to get everything prepared—not to mention the cost. Do you have any suggestions?

Author: Why not share the food costs and preparation with friends and family? I'll admit that I don't enjoy putting on a party but do enjoy getting together with family and friends. It can be so exhausting to get everything ready. I understand how Penney feels.

When guests offer to bring something, I let them. It makes the event less stressful for me. You might take care of the entree but ask your guests to bring an appetizer or dessert. Most people are glad to help out.

If you aren't comfortable with asking your guests to bring something, then simplify. Focus on the event and the time together and not on the food—you could serve finger foods or desserts only. No one will starve; just let them know before they come what you plan to serve.

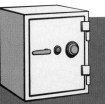

Bank On It

Dress up your dinner

Decorations can give your party that "wow" factor. Here are a few tips to dress up your next party:

- **Pick a theme color.** [Party supplies] come in all colors and the party looks more organized if you decide on a color.

- **Tablecloths.** You can use fabric from the fabric store, plastic or paper tablecloths from party stores. Make sure your tablecloths are not too long. You don't want your guests snagging on it and pulling the whole thing onto the floor.

- **Will your table have assigned seating?** This is something to think about too. If so...you can come up with some really cool ideas for place setting cards.

- **Kids tables.** Many restaurants put buckets of crayons and coloring pages out for kids. You could steal from this idea and do it too. Maybe add a few other things to the bucket if your party includes children.

- **Flowers and arrangements on tables.** [Tables] usually always have some type of centerpiece on the table. At the end of the party you can always raffle off the flowers on each table or give them away as parting gifts or party drawings.

- **Make sure your decorations are safe.** If you're using candles make sure they are melted in the holder so they don't fall out and start a fire. Better yet, use the battery candles instead.

"Party Planning Directory." Gone-ta-pott. Web, 10 July 2010 <http://www.gone-ta-pott.com/party_planning.html>.

Do The Math

$$\begin{array}{r} 2 \\ +\ 2 \\ \hline 4 \end{array}$$

One very expensive glass of wine

"Pearls seem to have been valued by peoples of all times…and there are many incidents in history showing the esteem in which they were held by the Greeks and Romans. The best known of these is probably Cleopatra's wager with Antony, that at a single meal she would swallow the value of a whole province." To that end, Cleopatra "is said to have dissolved a pearl of great value in a glass of sour wine," and then to have drunk the wine…. This story COULD be true if the pearl had first been ground into a very fine powder, added to the wine and then swallowed…." According to Pliny, a noted author of the time, wealthy Romans were accustomed to mixing pearls with their wine "to improve the flavor of the beverage."

So, pearl + wine = province.
Cleopatra wins!!

Adapted from: Farrington, O. 1903. Gems and Gem Minerals. Chicago: A.W. Mumford

Since we are talking about simplifying, and if it's about getting together and not about entertaining, then the "more the merrier" as far as I'm concerned.

Here are some of the most enjoyable parties that we've participated in:

One of our favorite get-togethers is a pot luck dinner. Everyone brings something—appetizer, entree or dessert, it always seems to work out. Everyone eats and then takes their dishes home to be washed. The perfect dinner—you make one thing to eat and enjoy eating many things. No mess, no fuss, and little effort for big reward.

A progressive dinner is lots of fun. The idea is to move from house to house for each course—start with appetizers at the first house, soup or salad at the next, your main course at another and dessert at the last house.

We had a large group participate in one of these progressive dinners. Some of the participants stayed home to host each course so as we arrived we took time to visit. You could also have a small group and everyone travels and enjoys the courses at each home. This is a great idea for neighbors or a group at a campsite.

Instead of preparing a big meal, I've put chili or soup in the slow cooker and served it with buns and a tray of veggies.

We also had an evening when the host provided cooked rice and everyone brought a topping for the rice. (It actually tasted better than it probably sounds.)

And how about *make your own sundaes* for dessert? Again the host supplied the ice cream and all the guests contributed their favorite ice cream topping. Who doesn't love a sundae?

My kids like to have a New Year's Day party where they sit around with friends and play games all afternoon and evening. I buy appetizers and finger foods and let them help themselves whenever they are hungry.

We've had games nights when all our guests just brought their favorite snack or dessert. No fuss and no hassle…

If you want to have company without all the work then try one of these simple party ideas.

Gift giving

Penny: We have a lot of friends and family and there always seem to be lots of birthday parties, weddings, showers and anniversary parties...It can get so expensive with all this gift giving. How can we lower our costs?

Author: Usually where there's a party, there are gifts. Of course you're right, it can get expensive. Maybe it's time to think "outside the box" (and yes, I did mean to be "p"unny).

If you choose to be creative and put your talents, skills and experience to good use, you can come up with great alternatives to traditional store bought gifts. We have a few suggestions for you but you can come up with lots of your own ideas!!

1. Make homemade gifts—preserves, breads, cookies, etc.

2. Give coupons for your time—housework, yard work, car washing, babysitting.

3. Offer to teach someone a skill you have.

4. Help with a home project.

5. Use a talent to create a gift—a drawing, a knitted item, crafts.

6. Prepare a favorite meal and/or dessert.

7. Write a letter or make a phone call.

Penny: You've got me thinking...

My mother-in-law Amy did not have much money, but she was one of the most generous people that I've ever known. She took her love of crafts and put it to good use—giving away hundreds of homemade items throughout her lifetime. In fact, at her funeral when her daughter asked for a show of hands for anyone who had received something homemade from Amy—quilts, afghans, mittens, scarves, sweaters, etc., almost everyone in the room raised a hand. Those gifts were meaningful because we realized how much time and effort went into making them.

Fool's Gold

Extravagant gifts for the girl who has everything

The chocolate lover. La Madeline au Truffe contains "a rare French Perigord truffle...surrounded by... rich decadent ganache; it is enrobed in Valrhona dark chocolate and then rolled in fine cocoa powder." Cost: $250 for 1.9 ounce.

The techie-girl. The Diamond Flower mouse...is made of 18-karat white gold encrusted with 59 brilliant-cut diamonds in the shape of a flower. The world's most expensive computer mouse (according to PC World) will set you back $25,000.

The social butterfly. The limited edition pink-iced Vertu Signature cell phone is made with 7.2 carats of pink and white diamonds set in 18-karat rose gold. Cost of the glitzy little must-have? A scant $73,000.

The trend watcher. Here's just what she needs...a Ruby Television, made by Opulent Items. The 40-inch HD flat-screen TV is encrusted with 155 fine red rubies cut in three different sizes to create a starry effect—the perfect ambience for movie nights. Cost: $75,000.

Regifting

Okay, you found the perfect gift for that special someone...the thing is, you found it in your closet, something that was given to you as a gift. You can leave it wrapped up in your closet for the rest of your life, dispose of it, give it away to someone who needs it, donate it to charity, sell it or regift it.

If you decide to regift, be sure to follow these regifting rules of etiquette from Jacqueline Whitmore, an etiquette expert and author of *Business Class: Etiquette Essentials for Success at Work*:

1. Only give a gift if it is in good condition. Be sure not to tamper with, open, or use the gift and keep all seals intact.

2. Regift in different social circles. Make sure the person receiving the gift doesn't know the person who originally gave you the gift. To avoid this mishap, label any gifts you don't intend to keep by jotting down when it was received and by whom.

3. The gift should be a good match. Before giving a recycled gift, ask yourself if the receiver will enjoy, appreciate and use the gift. If you're not sure, don't bother regifting it.

4. Remove the evidence. Before you regift, remove the original card that may be tucked inside the gift.

5. Retire unwanted gifts. Instead of regifting those items that you'll never use like that old bottle of cologne, canned ham, stale fruitcake, or itchy sweater...dispose of it so you and others will never have to see it again. (Whitmore, Jacqueline. "Regifting Etiquette: 5 Top Tips To Regift Gracefully." Etiquette Expert. 6 December 2009. Web, 10 July 2010 <http://blog.etiquetteexpert.com/regifting-etiquette-to-regift-or-not-to-regift/>.)

When you give a gift from the heart it won't matter if it's brand new, from the dollar store, homemade or a regift. If you choose a gift based upon the needs, wants and tastes of the recipient, it will be appreciated by the one receiving it.

Common Cents

"You know you are getting old when the candles cost more than the cake."

- **Bob Hope**

"We make a living by what we get, but we make a life by what we give."

- **Winston Churchill**

"For it is in giving that we receive."

- **Saint Francis of Assisi**

"The manner of giving is worth more than the gift."

- **Pierre Corneille, *Le Menteur***

We make these suggestions:

- Figure out the why, what, where, who and how of your party.

- Find the *perfect* location for your event.

- Decide how you will invite your guests.

- Decorate on a budget.

- When it comes to the food, share the work load.

- Find alternatives to traditional gift giving.

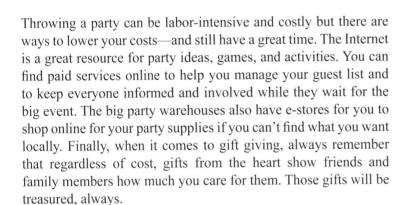

Throwing a party can be labor-intensive and costly but there are ways to lower your costs—and still have a great time. The Internet is a great resource for party ideas, games, and activities. You can find paid services online to help you manage your guest list and to keep everyone informed and involved while they wait for the big event. The big party warehouses also have e-stores for you to shop online for your party supplies if you can't find what you want locally. Finally, when it comes to gift giving, always remember that regardless of cost, gifts from the heart show friends and family members how much you care for them. Those gifts will be treasured, always.

Well, the party's over, but the fun goes on as we offer you some more reasons to celebrate. Come with us to the next chapter, where we'll show you that you don't need to be *brave* to enjoy the land of the *free*!

Money Talks

Have one's cake and eat it too

To *have one's cake and eat it too* is a popular English idiomatic proverb or figure of speech, sometimes stated as *eat one's cake and have it too* or simply *have one's cake and eat it*. It is most often used negatively, meaning an individual [using] a thing, and still attempting to benefit from or use it. It may also indicate having or wanting more than one can handle or deserve, or trying to have two incompatible things. The proverb's meaning is similar to the phrases, "you can't have it both ways" and "you can't have the best of both worlds."

"Have One's Cake And Eat It Too." Wikipedia, The Free Encyclopedia. Wikimedia Foundation, Inc. 7 July 2020. Web, 10 July 2010 <http://en.wikipedia.org/wiki/Have_one's_cake_and_eat_it_too>.

Okay, we may be stretching it when we use "have your cake and eat it, too" as the title for this chapter. (We do love the tie-in with cake in a chapter about throwing parties and entertaining.) However, we're also using the phrase to mean that you *can* have the best of both worlds when it comes to planning celebrations: save money and still give your guests—and yourself—a great time. Enjoy!

Web sites used in the chapter

http://bit.ly/cfn5Hy	(Gone-Ta-Pott.com) Types of parties and celebrations.
http://bit.ly/tww1	(Vista Print) "Make An Impression."
http://bit.ly/9uUPma	(SmileBox.com) Celebrate with fun party invitations!
http://bit.ly/bLR08k	(MoneyUnder30.com) "How Much Does An Average Wedding Cost?"
http://bit.ly/b2hCOi	(MyEvent.com) Why use a website to plan a party?
http://bit.ly/bEI3Ts	(PowerToChange.com) "The Top 10 Gifts You Shouldn't Buy Your Wife This Christmas."
http://bit.ly/cHk51u	(TheDigeratiLIfe.com) "How To Throw A Kid's Birthday Party Without Spending A Fortune."
http://bit.ly/9XXbjs	(Gone-Ta-Pott.com) Party decorating tips.
http://bit.ly/d65Wxs	(Farland.com) Some text about pearls.
http://bit.ly/d7oJS0	(CelebrateWithStyle.com) "Extravagant Gifts For The Girl Who Has Everything."
http://bit.ly/bZfoUe	(EtiquetteExpert.com) "Regifting Etiquette: 5 Top Tips To Regift Gracefully."
http://bit.ly/dBUVUz	(Wikipedia.org) A definition of "have one's cake and eat it too."

Additional resources

We're having a party

http://bit.ly/9INMIn	(Party411.com) "Life's A Party...But Not When You Spend Too Much!"
http://bit.ly/dDz7Kk	(MyPunchBowl.com) Free online party invitations and party planners.
http://bit.ly/9KhhFh	(About.com) "Plan A Party That Fits In Your Budget."

Keep it down (the cost that is)

http://bit.ly/9v4vmY	(Oprah.com) "How To Throw A Party On A Budget."
http://bit.ly/cqx52E	(WikiHow.com) "How To Plan A Party On A Budget."
http://bit.ly/btZYfd	(About.com) "How To Plan A Kid's Party On A Budget."

Gift giving

http://bit.ly/beKrMl	(FamilyEducation.com) "Saving On Wedding Costs."
http://bit.ly/bTP7OD	(MSN Money) "12 Rules For Regifting Without Fear."
http://bit.ly/ctR2Vg	(Squidoo.com) "20 Unique And Alternative Gift Ideas."

We asked, "How do you keep special occasion costs down?" and you said...

I make crafts/scrapbooks so I make my own gifts. I also make my own cards. I bake goodies as well and give them as gifts.

— **Jenn Gibson**

Whew! This is a toughie. I could skip the holiday entirely but my wife will not. We try to buy needful things, stuff for the house rather than trinkets for each other.

— **Warren Thaxter**

I buy items throughout the year. I recycle paper and cloth bags instead of using wrapping paper.

— **Audrey Stephenson**

When it is a BIG family...plan a dinner...and do a one name draw...to buy a gift.

— **Judith Samuels**

We don't go overboard with gifts for our kids or each other. We figure out a budget before the Christmas shopping begins and we stick to it. We draw names for an exchange between adult siblings and many times make gifts for them instead of buying them (although this doesn't guarantee that you will save money).

— **Joel Stoklosa**

I have gone to the dollar store before for birthday gifts for kids. I grab a little container and fill it with craft items. It can save you a lot of money. I have bought a lot of great gifts that way.

— **Terri Tyson**

Everyone in the family just draws one name from a hat and buys one $70 gift for that person instead of buying $40 gifts for everyone in the family. We really don't need more stuff anyway.

— **Dan Wood**

When I get together with friends we meet at someone's house and we all bring snacks or we chip in to buy pizza. We are just happy to watch movies together or to play games.

— **Michael J.**

Buy gifts throughout the year when things are on sale/least expensive.

— **Holly Norwick**

Buy gifts from work for cheaper than wholesale or mail something creative and personal using dollar store items.

— **Tara Streeter**

Look for items that are on sale or make your gift. There is nothing better than a gift made with love and memories.

— **Christine Horning**

Start shopping early, buy on sale, and do research on anything over $50. (Compare flyers.)

— **Dawn Lipop**

A lot of times I already know of occasions that will be coming up like the birth of a baby or a wedding. With so much notice given it is very difficult to *not* find a gift on sale somewhere. Lots of warehouse sales take place throughout the year. I will purchase them ahead of time so I don't have to overspend when the occasion comes along and then have to rush out to find something. I also like to go in on group gifts. Pooling money together can get a far better gift, often for less money. Knowing a craft also helps as you can make the gift—like knitting a hat and booties for a newborn baby.

— **Sue De La Franier**

Presents—I go to yard sales during summer and often find NEW items (still in their original wrappings) and give these as gifts at Christmas.

— **T. Thompson**

[I] budget how much [I] want to spend.

— **Anonymous**

I try to offer my talents/skills—like baby/wedding photography as a gift.

— **Jody Crane**

Warehouse outlet shopping and generally being aware of pricing [helps me to keep costs down].

— **Anonymous**

Chapter 11
Something For Nothing
GETTING FREE STUFF

"I don't care if it's free."

Money Talks

Don't look a gift horse in the mouth

Origin

From earlier "given horse": *"No man ought to looke a geuen hors in the mouth."* —John Heywood, 1546.

Horses' gums recede as they age making the teeth appear to grow long. Therefore, inspecting the teeth of a horse given as a gift would mean that [the] recipient is trying to see if the horse is old (undesirable) or young (more desirable).

The substitution of "gift" for "given" occurred in 1663 in Butler's *Hudibras*, because the iambic tetrameter required a shortening:

He ne'er consider'd it, as loth
To look a Gift-horse in the mouth.

Meaning

Do not unappreciatively question a gift or handout too closely.

"Don't Look A Gift Horse In The Mouth." Wictionary. Wikimedia Foundation, Inc. 19 June 2010. Web, 12 July 2010 <http://en.wiktionary.org/wiki/don't_look_a_gift_horse_in_the_mouth>.

In days gone by, many families had coats of arms, family crests and mottos. "The family's or individual's motto...[came] from the distinct 'battle cry' of an individual [or] perhaps it consisted of a favourite saying, or a heartfelt statement that gave the individual added mental courage going into battle. These too are unique and no two are shared, and were thus adorned upon the coat of arms, usually recorded in Latin." ("The History And Origin Of Heraldry." 4 Crests. Web, 12 July 2010 <http://www.4crests.com/hisandorofco.html>.)

Some of the family mottos are very inspirational, like these ones: *Data fata secutus—Follow the destiny allotted, Non nobis sed omnibus—Not for ourselves, but for all* or *Virtus sola nobilitat— Virtue alone ennobles.*

I'm sure this is all very interesting but you're probably wondering what it has to do with anything we've been discussing. Let me explain. When I was growing up our family had its own motto. I'm sure you'll also find it very inspiring: *If it's free, take it.* (It's actually much more inspiring in Latin: *Si haud sumptus usurpo— If no cost, take for oneself.*)

My father was what I term a "wheeler, dealer" so we followed this motto to a tee. Even if it wasn't something we wanted or needed, we took it because there was someone else out there who might want or need it and my father was sure to make a few dollars when he found that certain someone.

This tradition is very deeply engrained in me and even today I have a hard time refusing anything that is offered to me if it's free—even when I know I don't need it and can't think of anyone who might. That said, "one man's junk is another man's treasure" and sometimes it's just a matter of matching the item with the right person. In other words, you need to find the one who needs something that you want to give away or find the one who wants to give away something that you need.

Making connections/surf the net

The problem with the "get something for nothing" system is making the connection between person and item. Networking is a term that has become very popular nowadays when talking about business, but you were probably networking long before you heard the word. Look around you—you are surrounded by a *network* of family members, friends, business associates and acquaintances. When you are finished with an item—a piece of furniture or the exercise bike you no longer use—you probably look for someone who could use what you don't want anymore. Some people you know may be wondering what they can do with the computer they no longer need, a bike that's taking up room in the shed or the extra kitchen appliances. If you make it a practice to let the people on your own networking list know what you are looking for, you may find that they have just what you need, or know someone who does.

And if you feel like being more proactive and organized you might even set up your own exchange group (for clothes, toys, books, movies, sports equipment, exercise machines, etc.) with friends and family. You'll enjoy greater variety at lower costs. We've already given some ideas for this type of exchange in Chapter 8—ways to reduce leisure and entertainment costs. In Chapter 5 we talked about the *barter system*—trading time/goods/services—as another way to get free things.

When people move they usually try to go through their possessions and get rid of some of the things they no longer use. They may have a moving sale where prices are usually low because they are very motivated to get rid of as much as possible. They may not even want to bother trying to sell anything; they may just want to have things carted away by anyone who can use them.

Know anyone that's moving? This is a good time to mention what you are looking for. How many times have you seen big piles of *stuff* in front of a house when someone has just moved? It's better to take something you need and can use than to have it end up in the landfill.

Right On The Money

Recycling saves money

Selling recyclable materials offsets the extra costs of collecting and processing recyclables, making recycling the cheaper option for the community.

	Trash	Recycling
Collection	$60/ton	$70/ton
Landfill fees	$20/ton	—
Processing at recycling facility	—	$45/ton
Sale of material	—	$90/ton
NET COST	$80/ton	$25/ton

Plus, all the environmental benefits of recycling, such as reducing pollution and greenhouse gas emissions, have economic value as well—more than $55 per ton compared to landfilling.

Source : "Environmental Benefits Of Recycling." Eco-cycle. National Recycling Coalition. 2005. Web, 12 July 2010 <http://www.ecocycle.org/tidbits/ecocycletenreasons.pdf>.

Based on the recycling experience of the town of Loveland, Colorado in 2005.

Your Money's Worth

Get more from your reward programs

If you want to make the most of the reward program you have, follow these guidelines:

Pay your balance off at the end of the month. We've said it before; we'll say it again. If you keep a balance, you pay interest. If you pay interest, the value of any reward you earn is reduced or wiped out completely.

Reduce the number of cards you use, so that you accumulate more points/card. See the next point...

Don't spend your points right away as the rewards usually will get better as your points increase.

Watch out for annual fees as they take away from the value of the rewards you are trying to earn.

Look for opportunities to increase the rewards you earn. There may be bonus points available to be earned. You'll get to the reward faster and for less money spent.

If you can't handle credit then stop using your cards. The *free* rewards aren't worth the cost.

Have you ever heard of free yard sales? Several churches in our area have hosted these events. People donate what they no longer want and the community is invited to come and help themselves. These events are advertised in the community and often in the local paper so keep a lookout or organize one if nothing like that is available in your area. That'll show some community spirit!

And now if you've asked around and haven't had any success, you can be grateful for technology. Your "community" has just burst wide open. How about becoming part of a community that gives and gets items for free? Here's the introduction page on the FreeCycle website: "Welcome! The FreeCycle Network™ is...a grassroots and entirely non profit movement of people who are giving (and getting) stuff for free in their own towns. It's all about reuse and keeping good stuff out of landfills. Each local group is moderated by a local volunteer. Membership is free." ("Welcome." Free Cycle. Web, 7 August 2010 <http://freecycle.org>.)

Once you find your local community, and sign up to become a member you can post any items that you want to give away or look for items you want. Make sure that you are familiar with the rules of the group that you join before participating. It is not an exchange group—you give or you take, with no strings attached and no money changing hands.

Reward programs

How about shopping your way to free things? I remember when reward programs were a novelty. Our local department store began a *reward* program and issued *reward* cards with a corresponding *reward* catalogue to order from when you were ready to cash in your points. It was pretty exciting. Since I was going to be spending money anyway, I figured, "Why not get something for free out of it?" Now of course there are reward cards at the department stores and the pharmacy, the gas station and the grocery store. You can buy your groceries and earn air miles. You can earn points at the hardware store and use them to buy your groceries.

You can get credit cards that give you rebates on your gas purchases, earn you points for free movie tickets, pay for airline travel, earn you gift cards or even offer cash back on every purchase. It seems that everywhere you look there's another card with another reward program.

What do we think about all these programs? As long as you aren't over-spending to earn *free* items and if you pay credit card balances off each month (or better yet, as you spend), then why not? Personally, our family has eaten a lot of the points we've earned. Yummy!!

Bill: *So, with all the reward programs available, how do I choose the right program for me?*

Author: **Look for programs that award you points automatically—no coupons or phone-ins. Find something where the points are easy to redeem and they should offer something that's worthwhile to you. I don't want a card that gives me free movie tickets—I just don't go very often, but my husband loves it and uses his card all the time. I prefer to earn rewards that I can turn into food at the grocery store.**

Consider your needs and interests, and the way you spend your money—then you can find a card that fits your lifestyle.

Bill: *I guess I'll do some research.*

Author: **There are many websites that can help you find your perfect match. Check the additional resources section at the end of the chapter for some links to get you started.**

Putting a little effort into choosing the right card can be very rewarding!

Fool's Gold

I'll just have water

We can turn on our tap and fill up our glass with drinking water and it's virtually free. But apparently all water is not created equal.

The world's most expensive water can be found 2,000 feet down off the coast of Hawaii.

The name of this expensive water that is bottled by Hawaii Deep Marine is Kona Nigari.

This water is a seawater mineral concentrate that you mix with your regular drinking water.

The Japanese are driving the cost up even more as they cannot get enough. At this time, only 2 ounces of Kona Nigari costs $33.50 USD.

If you are thinking about purchasing one gallon then you had better be ready to charge it to get soaked— the price of one gallon is only $2,144.00 USD.

"World's Most Expensive Water." THE LONGEST LIST OF THE LONGEST STUFF AT THE LONGEST DOMAIN NAME AT LONG LAST. Web, 12 July 2010. <http://www.thelongestlistofthelongest stuffatthelongestdomainnameatlonglast.com/ expensive152.html>.

Freebies

Sometimes you'll find things that are free, period. On the CNN.com/living website, you can find a list of *surprising* free things: free education, free classes, free culture, free gyms, free photos, free pets, free phone services, free email reminders, free ice cream, free used books, free household items and free samples. Did you notice the one thing all those items had in common? Free! Free! Free! Is there more? Is there a catch? Check out the additional resources page for the website link to find out!

MSN Money (MoneyCentral.MSN.com) provides you with a list of free things in five different categories: financial services, entertainment, travel, advice and health care. Even the geeks (FreeStuffGeek.com) have a list of free items for you to consider including computer classes, comic books, CPR courses and music. Check the additional resources for the links to get the complete lists .

Many companies are willing and wanting to give you samples. (And then there are websites that organize these offers for you which makes it even easier.) You want to try new food products? How about make-up and beauty products? Need help with the laundry? How about diapers and a baby bag? Manufacturers want you to use their products and they are willing to send you samples, and sometimes coupons for you to use on your next purchase. What's the catch? You may have to do a short survey or register on the company website and, of course, it takes time. You have to decide if the free *whatever* is worth your time.

Mystery shoppers

You've probably heard of "mystery shoppers" who are hired by market research companies to check out the quality of service in restaurants, hotels and retail stores, etc. They make a purchase and are reimbursed for the cost of the item and usually allowed to keep the product in return for reporting on their experience. But because this is so appealing, it has been used by many crooks to scam the unsuspecting public who answer their mystery shopping "job" listings or pay for "certification" courses.

Don't get taken in. If you are interested in becoming a mystery shopper then check out the sidebar on this page to find more information.

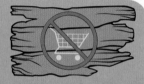

Buyer Beware

Mystery shoppers

If you are interested in becoming a secret shopper then follow these guidelines from the Federal Trade Commission website:

Becoming a legitimate mystery shopper for a legitimate company doesn't cost anything. Here's how to do it:

- Search the Internet for mystery shopping companies that are accepting applications. Legitimate companies don't charge an application fee. Many accept applications online.

- Do some homework about mystery shopping. Check libraries or bookstores for tips on how to find companies hiring mystery shoppers, as well as how to do the job effectively.

You can visit the Mystery Shopping Providers Association (MSPA) website at MysteryShop.org for information on how to register to be a mystery shopper with a MSPA-member company, a database of available jobs, and additional information on the industry in general. The MSPA also offers certification programs for a fee.

"The Secrets Of Mystery Shopping...Revealed." Federal Trade Commision. 6 July 2010. Web, 12 July 2010 <http://www.ftc.gov/bcp/edu/pubs/consumer/alerts/alt151.shtm>.

Nothing for something

We've looked at how you can get free stuff—*something for nothing*—but what if you have things you'd like to get rid of and you feel they still have some value for which you'd like to be compensated—*nothing for something*. Remember all our suggestions for getting good deals in Chapter 5? Well, now you are on the other side of the deal—the selling side.

Yard sale/secondhand stores/consignment stores

If you want to do the selling yourself, you can hold a yard sale. To be more successful, put in some effort beforehand. Let people know that you are having a sale. Public bulletin boards provide free advertising. You can post signs around the neighborhood or put an ad in the local paper. Listen to the weatherman to try to get a rain-free day. Just in case he's wrong, make sure that you prepare for bad weather—have items in the garage or under a canopy in case of rain. Clean and dust your sale items—if it looks better, it will sell for more. Make sure that you mark all the items so that customers don't have to ask the price. If you spread out your wares it will look like you have more and people will be more interested in stopping to look.

You can have family, friends and neighbors add their things to your sale or even better, you can organize a street sale to attract many more people.

If you're not the yard sale hosting type, where can you take your stuff? Secondhand retail stores will resell your sports equipment, video games, musical instruments, music, movies and clothing. They will pay you for your items if they think they can sell them. They want to make a profit so they will pay you accordingly. A consignment store will sell your items for you and pay you a portion of what it sells for or give you credit to use in their store. What they can't sell you can take back or donate to charity.

Online selling

Ready to venture online? You can advertise for free at ClassifiedAd.com, Kijiji.ca (Canada) or eBayClassifieds.com (USA) or CraigsList.com. Amazon.com will let you sell your items (for a fee) on their website—it's like a *cyber* consignment store. You can post your items on eBay.com for auction or on Half.com, its' non-auction sister site. There are even websites that specialize in a particular item such as Gazelle.com and SecondRotation.com for your electronics.

Factor This In

How to hold a garage sale

- Gather items for sale. Inventory them on a piece of paper.

- Assign a price and attach a label to each item.

- Tidy up your yard and garage.

- Make signs and advertise. [We suggest you use large print.]

- Have lots of table space.

- Organize your cash and have lots of change.

- Keep your display visibly attractive.

- Be an active seller and make sure you have lots of help.

- Negotiate with hagglers.

- Offer last-minute deals.

- Give away what doesn't sell.

- Take down your signs.

- Count your money.

Adapted from an article provided by Wikihow: "How To Hold A Garage Sale." Wikihow. 12 July 2010. Web, 12 July 2010 <http://www.wikihow.com/Hold-a-Garage-Sale>.

Give to charity

Penny: *I don't want to be bothered selling my old stuff. When I'm finished with it I just want it to go to a good home.*

Author: *I feel the same way. There are many charities that take clothing, furniture and household items. They sell these donations in their thrift store and use the money to help people in the community. Your generosity helps them help others.*

In turn, when you donate clothing and household items to places like Goodwill and Salvation Army you can ask for a donation receipt that will qualify for a tax deduction when you prepare your tax return.

When you donate items to a charity, you find a home for your unwanted items and the charity fills their store. They don't pay for your things but they make money when they sell them. You get a donation receipt and get some money back on your taxes. Someone buys the things you don't want for a good price. Win-win-win! Everyone is happy.

Penny: *That sounds like a good idea to me. It's time to do some spring cleaning anyway.*

Author: *Some of these organizations will pick up your donations right from your home. While they are always willing to take good used clothing and small household items, they may not have room for, or need, larger items. Check with them when you phone.*

Makes Cents

Online marketing

You have stuff and you want to get rid of it—why not make use of marketing options on the Internet? Here are some ways to do that:

1. Use your social network to sell to family, friends and co-workers.

2. Use online markets like Half.com or Amazon.com.

3. If items are hard to ship then list them on CraigsList , Kijiji. ca (Canada) or eBayClassifieds (USA).

4. Use auction sites.

5. Set up your own online store. Check it out at Amazon.com, eBay. com or Shopping.Yahoo.com.

6. Use a company to sell on eBay for you—like Bidadoo.com.

Giving to charity is a system that works for everyone! It may be time to look around your home for things you are no longer using that someone else can use.

We make these suggestions:

- *Network* with family and friends to find the things you need.

- Look online for free stuff.

- Find the right reward program for you.

- Enjoy the freebies that companies want to give you.

- Mystery shoppers beware.

- Someone wants your stuff when you are finished with it.

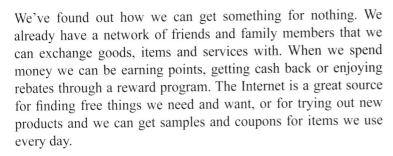

We've found out how we can get something for nothing. We already have a network of friends and family members that we can exchange goods, items and services with. When we spend money we can be earning points, getting cash back or enjoying rebates through a reward program. The Internet is a great source for finding free things we need and want, or for trying out new products and we can get samples and coupons for items we use every day.

When we've enjoyed the things we have and we are ready to pass them on, we can host a yard sale, sell them to a secondhand store or through a consignment store or list them online. If we don't want to sell our stuff, we can donate it to charity. We can ask for a charitable donation receipt in return. Everybody is happy.

And on that note, we move to our last chapter and explore the joy of giving...

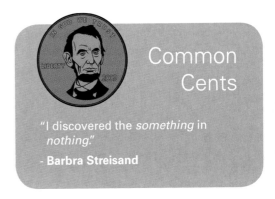

Common Cents

"I discovered the *something* in *nothing.*"

- **Barbra Streisand**

Web sites used in the chapter

http://bit.ly/bzvj1v	(4Crests.com) History and origin of coats of arms (heraldry) and mottos.
http://bit.ly/bp97qw	(Wictionary) A definition of "don't look a gift horse in the mouth."
http://bit.ly/9Idz9h	(EcoCycle.org) "Recycling Saves Money."
http://bit.ly/VVgu6	(FreeCycle.org) Free membership—find free things in your neighborhood.
http://bit.ly/bY1D2o	(TheLongestListOfTheLongestStuffAtTheLongestDomainNameAtLongLast.com) World's most expensive water.
http://bit.ly/bRLKUi	(CNN.com) 23 surprising things you can get for free.
http://bit.ly/b1YYHx	(Federal Trade Commission) "The Secrets Of Mystery Shopping…Revealed."
http://bit.ly/d9yvYE	(WikiHow.com) "How To Hold A Garage Sale."

Additional resources

Making connections/surf the net

http://bit.ly/bh7f31	(HowToConsign.com) Turning clothes into cash.
http://bit.ly/bEwh6p	(BusinessWeek.com) Most useful products and services available for free on the Web.
http://bit.ly/9qqI2J	(eHow.com) "How To Create A Local Online Barter Network."

Reward programs

http://bit.ly/9eRuLr	(NerdWallet.com) Check here for the best reward program for you.
http://bit.ly/9Nnze5	(MyPoints.com) Earn points and get rewards.
http://bit.ly/buw19F	(SmartMoney.com) Finding the best reward programs.

Freebies

http://bit.ly/a0PIr	(MSN) "13 Things You Can Get For Free."
http://bit.ly/c16NHf	(TotallyFreeStuff.com) Totally free stuff.
http://bit.ly/9VvbGu	(FreebieSample.com) Free samples.

Mystery shoppers

http://bit.ly/coYchE	(MoneyWatch) "Mystery Shopper Scam Alert."
http://bit.ly/94uSTW	(Mystery Shopper Job Finder) Start shopping for work today!
http://bit.ly/a2tiRo	(Mystery Shopping Guide) Get paid to shop and eat.

Nothing for something

http://bit.ly/bNllDq	(CraigsList.org) Sell with no fees.
http://bit.ly/b48kj8	(GoodHouseKeeping.com) "Turn Your Trash Into Cash."
http://bit.ly/cjfHcX	(ClassifiedAds.com) Free classified ads for cars, jobs, real estate, and everything else.

We asked, "What's the best thing you've ever got for free?" and you said...

The best thing we've earned is our reward miles which paid for us to visit our daughter for Christmas (and for myself to travel again to see her)—no blackouts, no restrictions on seats or airlines.

— **Barb Dousett**

It was an old kitchen cabinet that we got from someone's garbage. My husband refinished it and we used it for many years before we sold it to an antique dealer.

— **Shirley Durocher**

My wedding: I got the groom/groomsmen's tuxes, photographer, venues, tables/chairs/covers, and MANY accessories for free. The tux packages I won at a bridal show. (Girls, it's WORTH going to a couple of these before settling on vendors, etc.!!) All the other items I got from simply utilizing my connections: past employers, co-workers, friends, my church members and family...even my paper deliverer! Your connections can be very useful during events like this!

— **Ayla Lewis**

We got most of our furniture for free. Most of it was given to us by family but a few items we actually found during junk day. I have been able to find some solid wood furniture and refinish it to match what we had.

— **Blake Bowley**

The bench in my front hallway was free.

— **Rhona Bailey**

I have gotten some pretty good freebies out there but mainly due to networking skills. I think a good place to go for free things is someplace like FreeCycle.org. Everything listed there is free and no money can be exchanged. I managed to get an almost new serger sewing machine.

— **Sue Miller**

Our honeymoon!! We had our first night in the hotel paid for by a friend, and the next two nights at a bed and breakfast paid for by my mom....That was pretty cheap for us.

— **Chris Brunke**

I won a 2007 Grand Prix at a work open house.

— **Fred Johnston**

I found a burgundy leather sofa bed couch in great condition on the side of the road up the street from me. [There was] nothing wrong with it....Salvation Army wouldn't take it because there was a little rust on the sofa bed. I didn't see any. All good to me! Only reason they were getting rid of it was because they renovated and got a whole new set of furniture.

— **Anonymous**

My wife won a 46" plasma television at work in a raffle.

— **Ryan Johnston**

Almost every piece of furniture that we own was hand-me-downs from family or friends. We have armoires, trunks, bookshelves and beds! All it takes is a lick of paint or some elbow grease to make it your own. Think creatively about the object and see what can be repurposed: bookshelves into benches, armoires into computer stations, trunks as room dividers...

— **Dave Clarke**

One of our daughters travels a lot with her job and was building up too many sky miles. She offered us free plane tickets to anywhere we wanted to go. We went to Orlando, Florida to visit an aunt & uncle (and Disney).

— **Lee Dansie**

I work with children and seniors. I often talk to people about what I am doing. People have given me paper supplies and crafts that they no longer need for the children. I was given a great TV for movie nights for our youth group. Sharing your ideas and problems with others can lead to solutions that you may not have expected. People can be very generous when they see that their contributions have helped someone in need. I have been able to get guest speakers each month for my youth group for free because people usually enjoy helping young people.

— **Bonnie Wilson**

I won a contest on an Internet website. I earned points when people made purchases under my code on the website. Since I had the most points that month I won a guitar autographed by all the members of a band.

— **D. Johnston**

P.S. A few comments "by the people."

Chapter 12

It's Better To Give

GIVING, NOT GETTING

"Is this tax-deductible?"

Me, me, me, it's all about me, isn't it? It seems that we've spent almost the entire book talking about ourselves and what we can get. But life isn't just about what we can get; it's also about what we can give. Once you have your own finances in order you are in a better position to help others. And if you feel like one of the luckiest people on the planet, and we think you should, we say it's time to turn your focus elsewhere, away from you—the center of your universe.

Why do people choose to give? There are many reasons: to help those in need, to make a difference in someone's life, out of guilt, because there's a tax break—maybe perhaps just because it makes them feel good. Whatever the reason…we do think it goes without saying that there are many people in unfortunate situations—victims of natural disasters, disease, poverty and homelessness—that are in need of help. How and why you choose to share what you have is very personal. Whether or not you choose to give is your decision. For those who want to give, this chapter will look at some of the ways you can do that.

Karma

North Americans have adopted a philosophy of "what goes around comes around." Many of us believe that what we give out eventually will come back to us—whether good or bad. It's similar to eastern religions' teachings that what you do now will affect what happens to you in the future (or what you did in the past explains what is happening to you now). This is a very simplistic explanation of the concept of karma. Basically, the idea is that each person affects his own future and if he wants good things later he needs to give out good things now.

Charitable giving on a budget

The amount people donate varies widely. Some people pay tithing—10% of their income, and some just give a few dollars when someone knocks at their door. If you want to make charitable giving a regular part of your life, you can incorporate it into your budget and set up regular contributions through your bank. Charities need your contributions throughout the year, not just during the holiday season.

Money Talks

It's better to give than receive

Meaning

Just what it says…

Origin

Probably heard it from your mother. Her inspiration may have been the King James version of the Bible, Acts 20:35.

"I have shewed you all things, how that so labouring ye ought to support the weak, and to remember the words of the Lord Jesus, how he said, It is more blessed to give than to receive."

Keep in mind that you don't have to be rich to give. There are many ways to make a difference. If you are strapped for cash then..."here are a few ways to *give* when you have a limited budget:

- Give things you can make.

- Give your time.

- Give your patience.

- Give your compassion.

- Give your expertise." (Article provided by WikiHow, a wiki building the world's largest, highest quality how-to manual. Adapted from: "How To Be Generous On A Limited Budget." <u>Wikihow</u>. 26 March 2010. Web, 23 July 2010 <http://www.wikihow.com/Be-Generous-on-a-Limited-Budget>.)

Money isn't everything

If you don't have your own money to give, you can collect it from others by organizing a fundraiser—bake sales, auctions, book sales, etc. When I was a young girl our family hosted a fundraiser and held a carnival in our backyard for the neighborhood children. We had a great time doing it and then we donated the proceeds to the local hospital. When you donate other people's money, you are still giving.

But giving money is not the only way to help. Sometimes you can donate clothing, toys and household goods to charity. Some well known organizations collect these items and then sell them to a local thrift store. You can also donate food to a food bank. Many grocery stores have collection boxes in the store to make it easy.

Our church used to collect used stamps and soup labels. There's usually someone collecting pull tabs from soda cans. There may be bottle drives in your neighborhood as local groups try to raise funds. These items are converted into cash and then used to support good causes.

You can also go online and "click to give," at no cost to you (except a few minutes of your time). You will find a few examples on the following page. You'll see that "giving" has never been so easy.

Makes Cents

Ten practical tips to make your charity donations and contributions count for more

1. Be aware of the power of advertising.

2. Work with legitimate charities.

3. Look into tithing if you belong to a house of worship.

4. Include "charity" as part of your budget and tax planning.

5. Give charitable gifts for the holidays.

6. Choose your charities.

7. Verify that your donation is tax deductible.

8. How about trying your hand at fund raising?

9. Donate through online methods, without paying a dime.

10. Give your time.

Doyle, Stephanie. "Charitable Giving: How To Make Your Charity Donations Count For More." <u>The Smarter Wallet</u>. 10 November 2008. Web, 12 July 2010 <http://thesmarterwallet.com/2008/charitable-giving-how-to-make-your-charity-donations-count-for-more/>.

Look at these websites and what your click *buys*:

- FreeRice.com: rice

- BreastCancerSite.com: free mammograms.

- TheChildHealthSite.com: free child healthcare.

- TheLiteracySite.com: free books to needy children.

- TheRainForestSite.com: 11.4 square meters of rainforest habitat for wildlife.

- TheAnimalRescueSite.com: 0.6 bowls of food for rescued animals.

- EcologyFund.com: 70 square feet Rainforest, 4 pounds CO_2, 0.4 square feet U.S. Wilderness, 16.5 square feet Mexican Wildlife.

Do we have a volunteer?

Organizations also need your time, skills and talents. You can help in your own neighborhood. Do you have time to serve at a soup kitchen? Can you volunteer at your child's school? How about delivering for Meals on Wheels? Or you can participate in local beautification projects. You can find projects and volunteer opportunities in your own community.

Penny: I'd like to do more but my time is limited with a young family.

Author: If you want to volunteer but don't want to miss out on time with your family, then why not volunteer as a family? Do good and build family unity. Here are the top six ways to volunteer with your family from The Volunteer Family website: alleviate hunger, help someone stay warm, assist animals, make a child smile, clean the environment, and visit the elderly. (Information reprinted with permission from The Volunteer Family. "Family Volunteering Ideas." The Volunteer Family. Web, 8 August 2010 <www.thevolunteerfamily.org>.)

Penny: I guess it makes sense to include our children when we volunteer. I'll keep my eyes open for things we can do as a family.

Are you looking for volunteer opportunities on a larger scale? Volunteer Canada lists these categories for positions: marketing and communications, public relations, event planning, fund development, research, administration and technical support. Your experience and expertise can help out a favorite organization.

Are you ready to broaden your horizons and move outside of your own community? There are opportunities to volunteer not only in your own country, but also abroad. You can use your skills to make the world a better place. You've heard of Doctors Without Borders, the Peace Corps, the Red Cross, Salvation Army—all organizations that use volunteers to relieve suffering at home and around the world due to lack of medical care, natural disasters, disease, poverty, and homelessness. These are just a few of the many groups engaged in local and global projects.

Encore careers

On the Encore Career Institute website, you can read this explanation of the term *encore career*: "Do you want to launch a new career in the second (and best!) half of life? For many people, their main career motivation is to get to a place where they can disengage and be free from work. If, however, you feel that there should be, there MUST be larger goals in life than endless leisure, the Encore Career movement is full of people, just like you, who rather than looking for retirement, disengagement, and freedom from work, are looking for a new challenge, re-engagement, and freedom to work...freedom to work hours of their choosing; freedom to work in fields that fascinate them; freedom to work with people whose company they enjoy; freedom to utilize their unique knowledge, skills, and experience to make a difference in the world; freedom to follow their purpose and passion; [and] freedom to answer their personal 'calling.'" (Carnes, Joel. "Redefine Retirement, Redefine Yourself." Encore Career Institute. 15 September 2009. Web, 12 July 2010 <http://www.encorecareerinstitute.org/>.)

We couldn't put it any better. If you like this job description, this may be a "job" you want to work towards for your retirement years. Many people are taking the skills and experiences they've acquired throughout their working career and are using them to find self-fulfillment, while helping others, during their retirement years.

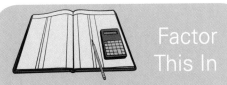

Factor This In

What are some of the things a volunteer can do?

- Coach a team.

- Read to children.

- Raise money for charity (fight diseases, reduce poverty, help the sick and injured, etc.).

- Care for the elderly.

- Feed the hungry.

- Provide counselling and support.

- Run errands and do deliveries.

- Gather and analyze data.

- Raise awareness of important issues.

- Do clean-up and repairs in the community.

- Build houses or playground equipment.

- Care for animals.

- Stage concerts, plays and other cultural events.

- Protect the environment.

- Plant trees.

- Help out with a political campaign.

"Volunteer Work." Youth Canada. 22 June 2010. Government of Canada. Web, 12 July 2010 <http://www.youth.gc.ca/eng/topics/jobs/volunteer.shtml>.

My brother's keeper

Fair Trade

Did you know that where you shop can also have an impact on people living on the other side of the world? "Fair Trade is an organized social movement and market-based approach that aims to help producers in developing countries and promote sustainability. The movement advocates the payment of a higher price to producers as well as social and environmental standards. It focuses in particular on exports from developing countries to developed countries, most notably handicrafts, coffee, cocoa, sugar, tea, bananas, honey, cotton, wine, fresh fruit, chocolate and flowers." ("Fair Trade." Wikipedia, The Free Encyclopedia. Wikimedia Foundation, Inc. 4 July 2010. Web, 12 July 2010 <http://en.wikipedia.org/wiki/Fair_trade>.)

Bill: I've heard about fair trade but don't know much about it.

Author: The idea of fair trade is to get the money directly to the people who are producing the crafts, goods and produce that we use here in our country. Too often, these workers are paid very little, while middlemen make a huge profit. Through the fair trade foundation, these producers are paid a fair price for their products.

"The Fair Trade Federation (FTF) is the trade association that strengthens and promotes North American organizations fully committed to fair trade. The Federation is part of the global fair trade movement, building equitable and sustainable trading partnerships and creating opportunities to alleviate poverty." ("Welcome To The Fair Trade Federation." Fair Trade Federation. Web, 7 August 2010 <www.fairtradefederation.org/>.)

The Fair Trade Federation website lists the members of their organization as well as the products that are available, categorized by country and item.

Bill: I'll take a look. It sounds like a good idea to me.

Child sponsorship

We've just talked about helping people in third world countries by the way we make our purchases. For a more personal involvement, and for about a dollar a day, you can sponsor a child, and help the child's family and community.

If you don't want the monthly commitment of sponsoring a child, organizations like World Vision and Plan allow you to purchase "gifts of hope." Your contributions purchase animals, literacy training, clean water, equipment, or plants—you can choose from a list of items. These practical gifts help communities to provide for the basic needs of their members but also allow individual families to have a fighting chance for independence.

If you don't want to participate in either of these options you can give a lump sum donation. You can choose to support a specific issue, fund a project or provide for emergency humanitarian needs—check online for more information.

Micro loans

There is another way to help the less fortunate. Kiva is an online loan facilitator that connects lenders with entrepreneurs. Kiva's goal is to alleviate poverty as entrepreneurs around the world are given loans to start their own small business. If you'd like to help you can provide a loan for as little as $25.

You become a business partner, not a donor: you lend money and the borrower pays it back. You give someone *the leg up* they need to escape the shackles of poverty—right from your home, over the Internet. Your small loan can change a life.

Give me a (tax) break!

Last and hopefully least, we should mention the tax perks of charitable giving. Your donations may qualify as tax deductions. Remember donations can be both monetary and non-monetary (clothing, household items, vehicles, stocks) so you can check a government website to see if the items qualify as a charitable donation.

We've given you some guidelines to use when contributing to charities. You want to make sure that the organization is legitimate. Unfortunately, there are many scams out there and getting involved in one helps no one but the crooks. But don't let the few "bad ones" stop you from helping the many good and worthwhile groups that exist.

Fool's Gold

Don't get caught in a charity scam!

1. BE WARY of every opportunity that presents itself—especially... in the wake of some big disaster that gets lots of media attention.

2. Ask for the name, address, and phone number of the charity—and whether or not it is registered.

3. Verify with the office of the charity that there is indeed a campaign going on, or that they've authorized the charity drive that you're being invited to contribute to.

4. Don't ever donate cash if you can help it. Write a check to the charity.

5. Ask what percentage of your donation goes directly to the cause. Get a receipt with the name of the charity on it.

6. Be especially cautious about getting a charity donation request by email.

7. Be especially wary about charities that claim to be raising funds for the local police or firefighters. Check with them first!

8. Don't give in to pressure or "guilt trips" about "suggested donations" or "requested minimum contributions."

9. The best way we know of to avoid charity scams is to decide IN ADVANCE which charities you'll support and CONTACT THEM...

Final words of wisdom

We want to end by sharing some words of wisdom from Benjamin Franklin. In a letter dated April 22, 1784, he wrote, "I do not pretend to give such a sum; I only lend it to you. When you... meet with another honest man in similar distress, you must pay me by lending this sum to him; enjoining him to discharge the debt by a like operation, when he shall be able, and shall meet with another opportunity. I hope it may thus go thro' many hands, before it meets with a knave that will stop its progress. This is a trick of mine for doing a deal of good with a little money." ("Pay It Forward." Wikipedia, The Free Encyclopedia. Wikimedia Foundation, Inc. 3 July 2010. Web, 12 July 2010 < http://en.wikipedia.org/wiki/Pay_it_forward>.)

The philosophy expressed in this letter is known today as "pay it forward." The phrase "pay it forward" became very well known after a book by the same name was released in 2000. Catherine Ryan Hyde, the author, explored the idea of repaying a good turn—paying back—by doing a good turn to someone else instead—paying forward....Though the book was a work of fiction, it inspired a worldwide social movement. In September 2000, Catherine Ryan Hyde helped create the Pay It Forward Foundation "to educate and inspire students to realize that they can change the world, and provide them with opportunities to do so." ("What Is The Pay It Forward Foundation?" Pay It Forward Foundation. Web, 7 August 2010 <http://www.payitforwardfoundation.org/>.)

Giving is not just about money; there are all kinds of ways to give. You can also contribute time, skills/talents and experience in your community, country and the world. You give as you can, when you can and how you can—right now and in the future. Service has no age limit. The need for volunteers is unlimited—with a little research you can find your perfect volunteer match. Though there can be tax benefits of donating to charity, we hope this isn't your main goal. There are a lot of other perks.

When you recognize how fortunate you are and you want to *give back*, then *pay it forward*. Look outside your own little world for ways that you can make our much bigger world a better place. There is need all around—you may have just what it takes to fill someone's need. Reach out and help someone today. You'll be glad you did and the world will be a little better because of it.

Your Money's Worth

Top 10 best practices of savvy donors

- Be proactive in your giving.
- Hang up the phone/eliminate the middleman.
- Be careful of sound-alike names.
- Confirm [charitable] status.
- Check the charity's commitment to donor's rights.
- Obtain copies of its financial records.
- Review executive compensation.
- Start a dialogue to investigate its programmatic results.
- Concentrate your giving.
- Share your intentions and make a long-term commitment.

"The 10 Best Practices Of Savvy Donors. Charity Navigator. Web, 12 July 2010 <http://www. charitynavigator.org/index.cfm?bay=content. view&cpid=419>.

We make these suggestions:

- What goes around, comes around.

- Charitable giving doesn't have to be expensive.

- You can give time, talents and means.

- Find your perfect volunteer "match."

- Look for the tax benefits of giving.

- *Pay it forward* instead of paying someone back.

We've come to the end of our journey. We hope you enjoyed the ride, got rid of some baggage that was weighing you down and have picked up some new and useful tools along the way. We've given you what you need to be successful as you continue on your own personal journey to reach your financial destination. We wish you a *bon voyage…*

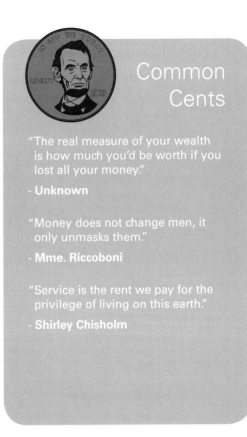

Common Cents

"The real measure of your wealth is how much you'd be worth if you lost all your money."

- Unknown

"Money does not change men, it only unmasks them."

- Mme. Riccoboni

"Service is the rent we pay for the privilege of living on this earth."

- Shirley Chisholm

Web sites used in the chapter

http://bit.ly/ahz8vG	(Wikihow) "How To Be Generous On A Limited Budget."
http://bit.ly/9XX71I	(TheSmarterWallet.com) "How To Make Your Charity Donations Count For More."
http://bit.ly/98MdlP	(TheVolunteerFamily.org) "Families Strengthening Communities."
http://bit.ly/auueaJ	(Idealist.org) "Volunteering With Your Family."
http://bit.ly/cIaD3d	(EncoreCareerInstitute.org) "Redefine Retirement, Redefine Yourself."
http://bit.ly/9zI9rK	(Youth Canada) Volunteer work suggestions.
http://bit.ly/9qaoAb	(Wikipedia) A definition of "fair trade."
http://bit.ly/arIkt	(Fair Trade Federation) Creating a just economic trade system.
http://bit.ly/bMN914	(FeedingAmerica.org) "Hunger And Poverty Statistics."
http://bit.ly/ZS3o	(Kiva.org) Micro loan program.
http://bit.ly/br6QNt	(Scambusters.org) Protect yourself from scams.
http://bit.ly/bZfDrC	(Wikipedia) A definition of "pay it forward."
http://bit.ly/cAZbf3	(Pay it Forward Foundation) You can change the world.
http://bit.ly/bEnSuQ	(CharityNavigator.org) "Top 10 Best Practices Of Savvy Donors."

Additional resources

Charitable giving on a budget

http://bit.ly/bc9GRG	(GlobalGiving.org) Give to the causes and countries you care about.
http://bit.ly/9NNNZK	(JustGive.org) Donate online and be an informed giver.
http://bit.ly/aPwTEw	(MicroGiving.com) Donate tiny contributions to charity from your computer.

Money isn't everything

http://bit.ly/9Yap8a	(Charitable Gift Giving) "Gifts That Help."
http://bit.ly/bkfIkU	(Care2.com) Click to donate—free clicks generate donations for your favorite causes.
http://bit.ly/aVsZ9i	(TopTenz.net) 10 best creative charity websites.

Do we have a volunteer?

http://bit.ly/cLL9D3	(Canadian Living) "Volunteering 101." How to give back to your community.
http://bit.ly/bIQ4Fb	(CreateTheGood.org) Volunteer opportunities in your community.
http://bit.ly/do1EH1	(Idealist.org) Find world-wide volunteer opportunities.

Encore careers

http://bit.ly/amPZMv	(Encore.org) "Find Your Encore Career."
http://bit.ly/aJnNjZ	(SmartMoney.com) "Switching Careers At 50, Boomers Look For Fulfillment."
http://bit.ly/J4S4U	(BusinessWeek.com) "How To Discover Your Encore Career."

My brother's keeper

http://bit.ly/dkS41a	(Pay It Forward Foundation) Changing the world one favor at a time.
http://bit.ly/bgVSas	(ArticleOnlineDirectory.com) "Helping Others Succeed Financially."
http://bit.ly/aJX83D	(CollegeCentral.com) "Key Questions Before Helping Others."

Give me a (tax) break

http://bit.ly/9wCpNH	(USA) (SmartMoney.com) "The Tax Perks Of Charitable Giving."
http://bit.ly/c4HXHl	(USA) (CharityNavigator.org) "Tax Benefits Of Giving."
http://bit.ly/cVB7eT	(Canada) (Canada Revenue Agency) Giving to charity: Information for donors.

We asked, "What is one way you help others—charitable giving?" and you said…

We give to the humanitarian fund at church, donate food and drive people (who are unable to get there on their own) to appointments.

— **Alberto Bonini**

I made donations through work—they came out of my pay automatically.

— **Diane Chisholm**

I participate in charity runs and donate money to charity for causes. We pick causes and decide with our budget how much we can afford to give. We also donate clothes, household items and time.

— **Mary Jane Conboy**

I collect used bicycles and computers for donation to the local homeless drop-in center that has several programs in place to recondition these items and to redistribute them to low-income families. I have friends drop off old computers so that I can repair them. I then donate them to single mothers through friends of mine that have a social services agency.

— **Ken Norwick**

At Christmastime when my children were young we used to take some money and drop it off at the home of someone we thought could use it. The kids would knock on the door and run. It was a blast.

— **M. B.**

We have a foster child. We give to local and international charities. We feed people and we share what we have with others.

— **Deborah Holt**

I volunteer at community and church activities as well as donating approximately 12% of our income to church and charities.

— **Don Turnbull**

Apart from giving money, try to become aware of needs. Help when you can. I have a little saying that has motivated me for years, "A little help is worth more than a lot of sympathy."

— **Catherine Matthews**

I help organize a large charity hockey event for the Heart & Stroke foundation. We raise over $130,000 annually with the *Hockey for Heart* tournament.

— **Louise Weir**

I give charitable donations through my church where 100% of those donations go to the needy.

— **Kirk Bailey**

We sponsor two children through World Vision.

— **Glenn Davies**

We help at a soup kitchen, donate to humanitarian relief, volunteer at Boy Scouts, and give our time at church.

— **David Charlesworth**

Have your children support a child as a family and let them contribute a few cents of their own money to the monthly fee—make sure you make a big thing of collecting it each month. Talk about the child's life. Your children can also write or send pictures to the child occasionally. [On the home front] it's nice to do little parcels for shut-ins at Christmas, this can involve the kids doing cards, etc. or making little beaded bracelets, etc.—nothing expensive, but thoughtful.

— **Gail Cain**

I try to buy tickets to the circus every year and donate the tickets to under-privileged children.

— **Sherry Dallin**

P.S. A few comments "by the people."

Afterword

I've spent most of my adult life working at jobs that were connected in some way to money. I started as a bank teller, then went into tax preparation and finally into financial planning. I decided that I would like to write a book about cash management and how to spend money better so I approached some friends, Eric and Robin Poulin, to propose a joint project. They run their own budgeting software company and are the most disciplined money managers I've ever met. At the same time that I had my great idea, they had also been thinking about writing a book and were wondering who they could work with. Apparently, "great minds think alike" (we flatter ourselves) and we decided to join forces and thus the partnership was formed.

I have to speak for myself here: I've made some good money decisions in my life and even some *really* smart ones. I've also made some big mistakes. There are things I've learned over the years and some things I wish I had known earlier. Researching this book has reinforced my confidence in my good money habits and also given me many new insights. I've learned many great ideas from others as I've read the responses to our survey questions.

We know that if you will read this book and apply the techniques we've suggested that you will be able to learn from our mistakes and avoid many of the pitfalls that your friends and neighbors are falling victims to. When you look at the statistics for personal household debt and bankruptcies, you know that help is needed.

We've taken what can be a daunting subject and made it easier to understand and (dare we hope?) fun— well, at least interesting. We've covered cash management basics on the topics of budgeting, emergency planning, credit and debt, saving and investing, how to find a good deal and how to teach children money skills. We believe that a little knowledge goes a long way. We've also included money saving ideas in specific categories, like food, travel, gift giving and celebrations. We included tips to help you shop online safely and gave some suggestions about how to make money on the things you no longer need. Through our research, we've found many resources for money saving ideas from the Internet, magazines and television programs, and now we pass them on to you.

We've given you the tools you need to be successful and we expect that you will want to use them. We want to remind you that it is important that you make your *financial matters*, a *family matter*. You want to be on the same page as your spouse or partner when it comes to making money decisions. We recommend that you work together as a family. Then we encourage you to ***power spend***—to spend less and get more—with your hard earned dollars.

Additional Resources

There is a lot of information available today on a wide variety of money topics. We don't claim to know everything about money, but we've gathered information from many sources and put it together into a book for your easy reference. We know that you are just as capable at searching the web to find answers to your money questions as we are but we know that *time is money* so we've done some of the work for you. You'll get the information you need without having to use up your valuable time.

The sidebars on every page contain great information related to the chapter topic. However, in most cases, what you read there is just a summary or a small part of what is available on the website we used as our information source. If you decide that you need clarification on a topic, or just *have* to know more, you will find the source of the article at the bottom of the sidebar and the link to it on the additional resources page at the end of the chapter.

We've mentioned a lot of websites throughout the book—and there are many more that we want to share with you. We just don't have enough room to put them all in the book. But don't despair—there is a way!!

Here's our solution: we are providing you access to our Power Spending website: PowerSpendingBook.com. You'll see that the website is full of additional resources for every topic in every chapter. You'll also find more responses to our survey questions—so you see how others have applied successful money techniques in their lives, and you'll read about their best deals and even some of their money mistakes. You'll find all the information divided by chapter headings, and then again by the chapter subheadings.

And if you find that we're missing a great website that fits into one of our topics, we invite you to send us the link. We'll check it out. We'd also like to hear your stories. Let us know how you use your money (you can even confess your money mistakes) and share your great ideas with us. When you apply the techniques you've learned in this book, let us know about the results—what worked and what didn't. Let us know what you have learned. You will find that it is easy to send your ideas, stories and experiences to us on our website.

Our goal is to provide you with a book and website that you will be able to look to as valuable resources when you are making money decisions, looking for money saving tips or just want some "tried and tested" methods for making your money go further. Let us know how we're doing, and how *you're* doing!

Sidebar Index

Index

About the Authors

Carolyn Johnston is a Certified Financial Planner with a longtime interest in both financial matters and in writing. This book is where those two interests have come together. Carolyn is married (27 years and counting) and a mother of four adult children and has had lots of practice in finding ways to manage money effectively. Besides reading and writing, Carolyn also loves to garden and research personal family history in her spare time.

Eric Poulin is the CEO and cofounder of Calendar Budget Inc. and the developer of CalendarBudget®, an online personal finance manager that makes it easy to track your money and reach your financial goals. Eric learned principles of cash management from his parents at an early age, studied more on the topic, and now helps others implement these principles through CalendarBudget®. Eric is the father of 5 girls and loves seeing them learn and succeed.

Robin Poulin is Vice-President of Business Development and cofounder of CalendarBudget Inc. an online personal money management tool. As a mother of 5 young children she is always looking for ways to save money and find great deals. She knows how to get more for her money! Robin's passion is people—helping them find success as they set their goals and work towards achieving them.

About the Illustrator

David Johnston is a graphic designer/illustrator. This is his second book—he also illustrated a children's fitness program book. When he was asked (the inevitable question) at age 5, "What do you want to be when you grow up?" he replied, "An artist." His answer has never changed over the years. After high school he attended a three year college program to learn the graphic design trade and has been working in that field ever since.

The easiest and fastest way for us to get your book to you is by ordering online through our website: PowerSpendingBook.com. We realize that everyone is not comfortable placing an order online so we are also offering a mail order service. You can fill out the order form below and send it to: *A Better Choice Publishing*, 41 Temperance Street, P.O. Box 2, Clarington, ON L1C 3A0, Canada or fax it to us at 1-888-700-8414.

If you want to order 5-10 books (oh, please do!), we will say "thank you very much" by covering the shipping costs for you. For those who wish to order even more copies, please contact us at 1-888-700-8414 to find out about our discount schedule.

MAIL ORDER FORM

Please send me _____ copies of **POWER SPENDING** @ $22.95 each
(I understand that I may return it for a full refund—for any reason, no questions asked.) _____

Canadian residents add 5% GST _____

Postage and handling: $3.50 for 1 book, $1.75 for each additional book
(up to 4 books, for 5-10 or more books see above) _____

Total Amount Enclosed _____

Enclosed is my: check ☐   money order ☐

Name _____

Address _____

City _____   State/Province _____

ZIP/Postal Code _____   Country _____

Phone _____   Email _____

Make all checks or money orders payable to *A Better Choice Publishing*.

Give a gift that makes a difference

Power Spending: Getting More For Less is a great gift for high school and college graduates, young adults, newlyweds, and new parents. It is a gift that would be appreciated for birthdays, graduations, wedding showers or at Christmas/holidays.

We can send the book directly to the "chosen ones" if you also include their names and addresses on a note enclosed with your order.

The easiest and fastest way for us to get your book to you is by ordering online through our website: PowerSpendingBook.com. We realize that everyone is not comfortable placing an order online so we are also offering a mail order service. You can fill out the order form below and send it to: *A Better Choice Publishing*, 41 Temperance Street, P.O. Box 2, Clarington, ON L1C 3A0, Canada or fax it to us at 1-888-700-8414.

If you want to order 5-10 books (oh, please do!), we will say "thank you very much" by covering the shipping costs for you. For those who wish to order even more copies, please contact us at 1-888-700-8414 to find out about our discount schedule.

MAIL ORDER FORM

Please send me _____ copies of **POWER SPENDING** @ $22.95 each
(I understand that I may return it for a full refund—for any reason, no questions asked.) _____

Canadian residents add 5% GST _____

Postage and handling: $3.50 for 1 book, $1.75 for each additional book
(up to 4 books, for 5-10 or more books see above) _____

Total Amount Enclosed _____

Enclosed is my: check ☐   money order ☐

Name _____

Address _____

City _____   State/Province _____

ZIP/Postal Code _____   Country _____

Phone _____   Email _____

Make all checks or money orders payable to *A Better Choice Publishing*.

Give a gift that makes a difference

Power Spending: Getting More For Less is a great gift for high school and college graduates, young adults, newlyweds, and new parents. It is a gift that would be appreciated for birthdays, graduations, wedding showers or at Christmas/holidays.

We can send the book directly to the "chosen ones" if you also include their names and addresses on a note enclosed with your order.